Linda Neil is an Australian writer, songwriter and documentary producer. Her first book, *Learning How to Breathe*, was published in 2009 to wide acclaim. She has a PhD in creative writing and has taught creative writing, cultural and media studies, and film and television at the University of Queensland. Trained as a classical violinist, Neil has performed with orchestras and rock bands, and recorded and toured with some of Australia's leading independent artists. Her radio documentaries have been shortlisted for the United Nations Association of Australia Media Peace Awards (*The Asylum Seekers*, 2004) and awarded Gold and Bronze medals at the New York Festivals (*The Long Walk of Brother Benedict*, 2011, and *The Sound of Blue*, 2008), and her script for *The Long Walk of Brother Benedict* was also nominated for best documentary script at the 2011 Australian Writers' Guild Awards.

http://lindaneil.bandcamp.com/releases

Praise for *Learning How to Breathe*

'Neil writes with her mother's gift for song and her father's gift for poetry ... A talented storyteller.' *The Sydney Morning Herald*

'A fine and sensitive writer ... Linda Neil has honoured her mother with exceptional storytelling, and set a high standard for future Queensland, and Australian, literature.' *The Courier-Mail*

'In a substantial and musical memoir, skilfully orchestrated and beautifully cadenced, Neil explores the lives of her family from grandparents to grandchildren ... Often angry, Neil's memoir is nevertheless both engaging and informative, written with tenderness, imbued overall with love.' *Adelaide Advertiser*

'This memoir is distinguished by a dignified and consistent voice ... a sharpish sensibility that never falters and, what's more important, never dissolves into mawkishness.' *The Age*

'A virtuoso performance.' Amanda Lohrey

'Finely crafted, subtle and tender, *Learning How to Breathe* is a beautiful tribute to the loving complexity of family. It reminds us that inspiration lies at the heart of both intimacy and art.' Gail Jones

'A superb memoir – moving, transporting, unforgettable.' Marion Campbell

All
Is
Given

A Memoir in Songs

LINDA NEIL

UQP

First published 2016 by University of Queensland Press
PO Box 6042, St Lucia, Queensland 4067 Australia

www.uqp.com.au
uqp@uqp.uq.edu.au

Cover design and illustration by Alissa Dinallo
Typeset in 11.5/16 pt Adobe Garamond Pro by Post Pre-press Group, Brisbane
Printed in Australia by McPherson's Printing Group

Earlier versions or extracts of these pieces have been previously published: 'Spike and Me:
A Fantastic Adventure', *Meanjin*, vol. 60, no. 2, 2001. 'Bahut Acha in Bharatpur', *M/C
Reviews*, 25 May 2008; *extempore*, no. 5, November 2010; and Rick Hosking and Amit
Sarwal (eds), *Wanderings in India: Australian Perceptions*, Monash University Publishing,
Clayton, Vic., 2012. 'The Flower Lady of Zhongshan Park', *Shanghai Daily*, 12 December
2011. 'Singing Love Songs in Kathmandu', *Molossus*, 19 December 2011. 'On Kindness in
Kolkata', *Sunday Life*, 1 February 2015.

Australian Government

This project has been assisted by the Australian Government through
the Australia Council, its arts funding and advisory body.

This project has also been assisted by an AsiaLink Arts Residency
with the Shanghai Writers' Association.

National Library of Australia
Cataloguing-in-Publication data is available at http://catalogue.nla.gov.au

ISBN
978 0 7022 5409 3 (pbk)
978 0 7022 5732 2 (ePDF)
978 0 7022 5733 9 (ePub)
978 0 7022 5734 6 (Kindle)

With love to all my family and friends
at home and around the world

Contents

Prologue: Songbook

The woman with the blood-red lips stood in front of me, hands on hips, blocking my way into the kitchen. I didn't feel like talking. At least not till after I'd eaten. And I usually didn't eat till after I'd finished singing. As my house concerts sometimes ended at 11 pm, I often had dinner just before midnight.

It had been one of those evenings and I was starving.

The woman looked colourful and determined. Her voluptuous, well-nourished body was draped in crushed velvet, her earrings were shaped like pink cherries, her hair was the colour of chocolate. In my famished state I could've taken a bite out of her.

I leaned forward, squinting at her necklace, which consisted of tiny lettered cubes strung together. They spelled out a name: Luciana.

Tell me about your loves, Luciana purred. *Your many, many loves.*

The host of that evening's concert waved a drink and a plate of food at me from across the room. I nodded gratefully, wondering how I could politely excuse myself, find a quiet spot and eat.

Your Indian love, your Jewish love, your French amour. Luciana ticked them off like items on a United Nations shopping list.

I could tell she wanted to start an in-depth conversation. But I'd been singing and telling stories for nearly three hours and I was exhausted.

Concerts can be like that – they can leave you spent, but at the same time they energise the people who've listened to you. The intimacy of house concerts, what I call lounge-room concerts, heightens that relationship. Without a stage or a microphone to separate the singer from the audience, a concert of love songs can feel particularly autobiographical. Less a performance than an embrace.

My host finally came to my rescue. He introduced me to Luciana – *no*, she laughed, *that's not my real name* – who hugged me and thanked me for the concert.

Mind if I sit with you while you eat, she asked. *I want to find out the real stories behind the songs.*

We found some cushions and lounged on them beside the glowing fire. In the orange light I noticed that Luciana had the kind of beauty that once would have made me collapse with envy. But since I'd started writing my own songs, my own music and lyrics, I'd realised that beautiful things also came from within and it was better to spend time excavating those things than dwelling on what I lacked. In that way making music made me move easier in the world.

I prepared to offer excuses as to why I didn't feel like giving any more of myself while I ate. I needn't have worried though. It wasn't discovering the details of my life that Luciana was interested in, but the telling of hers. What I had shared had only temporarily focused attention on me and my stories; this had in turn stimulated her memory and reflection.

It was one of the gifts – and surprises – of these concerts: to experience the spirit of another as it wakened and found a way to be articulated. So as I munched on garlic bread and a variety of dips and spreads, Luciana shared with me the stories of her life, her travels, her growth and trans-formations and all her loves, as if she were the singer of a hundred marvellous songs and I were her hungry audience. I never thought to ask her if all her stories were true. I just enjoyed her pleasure in their telling.

People often think songs, especially love songs, are auto-biographical. In my experience, they may well be inspired by real people but the form of a song means that, from this basis of fact, changes need to be made. A bass line is added perhaps. Something high is included. A man becomes a woman. A five-letter name expands to eight, night becomes day. A memory becomes a melody, a moment of potential becomes a love song.

As my wise friend Sophie says, the facts may not all be true but the feelings certainly are. And if some events depicted did not happen exactly the way they are described, perhaps they should have. A fantasia and a theme and variations are other musical forms that improvise and embellish simple melodic phrases. JS Bach did it most famously in the *Goldberg Variations*, and he was also famous for his prowess at royal gatherings, where he would improvise a dozen variations on a theme designated by his royal host – in record time.

So think of this collection of stories as a book of songs that contains improvisations and variations on themes of truth. If you listen closely enough you might even be able to hear the fabric of facts and fiction as they are stitched together. What they create when integrated may not be entirely fact or fantasy but something exploratory and hybrid – factitious or fictual – and writing them has been as delightful as making a song. I hope you can listen as you read and hear all the harmonies and overtones that surround music, the same way I have listened as I write.

Spike and Me:
A Fantastic Adventure

It all started in Brisbane and ended up across the other side of the world. Stories can be like that. If you wait long enough, they start to unfurl with the rhythm of Greek myths. If you look closely enough, you can almost see the paper they're written on as a map of words; one tiny scratch marks the humble beginnings of a long, sometimes magical tale that traverses countries and oceans. Journeys always seem to take you out of the small, into the large, and then back again. Not that I thought Brisbane was small – well, actually I did; everyone did at one time or another. But these days I like to sing its praises; to see, in its tiny, seemingly insignificant local events, the roots of greater, more fabulous possibilities. That's how it turned out in my life anyway.

I once read to a blind person. She lived down the road from us in Warren Street, St Lucia, during my last year at school. Her name was Mrs Featherington, although, in the teenage tradition of shortening everything, I referred to her as Feathers. Feathers was studying law at the University of Queensland and also learning singing from my mother.

One summer, during a particularly vocal discussion with my siblings around the dinner table, Mum suddenly leaned towards me and said: *If you like the sound of your own voice so much, go down the road and read to Mrs Featherington.*

I found out later that Mum had already volunteered me as one of Feathers' small band of readers, who called at her house to read law books, legal briefs, university texts and the Bible.

Oh God, I remember pleading. *Don't make me read the Bible! I'll do anything, just not the Bible!*

So I was put down on the list marked 'miscellaneous', which meant I was reading for entertainment and not educational or religious purposes.

My father suggested I choose reading material with *some* literary merit and handed me a book by Katherine Mansfield. Mum countered with the offer of a biography of Dame Nellie Melba (or was it Joan Sutherland?), which she assured me was a 'jolly good read'. But I rejected any notion of highbrow pursuits during my holiday and chose instead a copy of *Adolf Hitler: My Part in His Downfall* by Spike Milligan.

I can't say I looked forward to visiting Feathers in my allotted time. She'd always struck me as a crabby sort of woman. And even though Mum would ask me how *I* would be if I couldn't see, when it was hard to get a civil word out of me even with all my faculties intact, I still thought it was a tiresome chore. So I rocked up to Feathers' doorstep and entered her dark but tastefully furnished residence, with a lot of resentment and very little hope of having a good time.

Two pages into Milligan's book, though, Feathers and I were in fits of giggles. By the fifth or sixth page, the giggles had turned into guffaws and snorts of laughter. This symphonic hilarity continued throughout Spike's story. I can't recall much about the content of the book now, or even the tone. What I do remember is that by the time I had finished reading the book, which coincided with the completion of my rostered duty as a volunteer, Feathers and I had bonded in a way no amount of talking one on one could have achieved. It was as if our shared laughter had bridged the chasm between our personalities. As if every time Feathers had stopped me mid-sentence and spluttered *no, no, read that bit again* because the sound of her giggles had drowned out the previous words, we had become members of some secret society of laughers.

A few years later, while I was living in London, I switched on BBC Radio and suddenly there was Spike himself, or should I say Spike's voice itself, on a program called *In the Psychiatrist's Chair*. I'd never heard Spike speak before, except for on the old *Goon Shows* my dad used to chuckle over on Saturday afternoons. I was surprised by the sadness and resignation in his natural voice. And if, as the cliché says, your heart can go out to someone, that night my heart went out to Spike as he talked about his breakdowns, his manic episodes and the catastrophic effect his illnesses had had on his family.

I don't know whether it was the mood of the midnight hour or just the pain in Spike's voice, but I found myself in the early hours of the next day writing him a letter about my reading adventures with Feathers. I remember stumbling over some strange observation about how books are sometimes more than just formations of words organised into coherent communication, and can become things that pass between people, like happiness or love.

The next day, still buoyant from the previous evening, I walked down to the post office, happy that I had enough follow-through to finish *and* mail Spike's letter. The London sky, usually threatening rain, was startlingly blue that day; it sent down through my body that little ache which coldness and brightness can produce in Antipodean flesh.

I'd addressed the letter to Spike care of the BBC and released it to the Royal Mail with little expectation that he would ever receive it, let alone read it, but satisfied that I hadn't left my thoughts unsaid (or unwritten) as I had left so many things undone in my life up to that point.

For some reason, I wasn't surprised or even that excited when, two weeks of London life later, I received Spike's reply. There was a sense of *fait accompli* about my reaching out to Spike and his replying. The tone of the letter was one of kindness and a sort of exhausted gentleness. He said how much my letter had meant to him. Not just that I'd written it, but *how* I had written it. Not as a fan, he said, but as another human being, responding not to his achievements but to his suffering. I wasn't aware that was how I had responded to him. Reflecting on it now, I think Spike was looking for something and he thought, through my letter, that he'd found it, no matter what my actual intent had been. Perhaps I was looking for something too: a connection with someone I admired – a writer, a comic, an inventor – whom I never dreamed it would have been possible to meet back in Warren Street. Receiving Spike's letter seemed to signal a change in my destiny and I was ready for that change.

*

Further correspondence followed. Our contact seemed natural to me. So when he suggested we meet for dinner, the only counter-suggestion I had was that, as my experience of eating in London was limited to the cheapest, nastiest, greasiest takeaway available, namely the Chinese diner down the road where you could still get egg fried rice for one pound, we rendezvous at a restaurant of his choosing.

We met at one of Spike's favourite Indian restaurants, a little out-of-the-way diner in a side street of Notting Hill, called The Tandoori Traveller. During dinner, as we shared dishes of rogan josh, chicken korma and dal saag washed down with Heineken and Foster's lager, our conversation ranged over a wide variety of subjects. Spike himself had made some kind of list on his serviette, to which he referred every now and then. I don't know why he felt the need to take notes, although once or twice he confessed to a fear that he was a potential candidate for Alzheimer's. But to me, despite, or perhaps because of, the small quantity of food that he spilled onto his chin during dinner, he seemed as carefree and buoyant as a young man. In fact, at times I found his dishevelled appearance, even his sadness, strangely attractive.

From what I can recall, here is a small list of some of the topics we covered during our spicy dinner.

1. The Goons
2. Goonishness
3. The listing of Goonishness in some future dictionary
4. Some future dictionary of Goonishness
5. Dirty English cutlery
6. Woy Woy
7. Wyong
8. Woop Woop
9. Doo-wop

10. Doolittle
11. Do as little as possible
12. Doing too much
13. Breakdowns
14. Things that make Spike sad
15. Things that make me sad (which included things making Spike sad)
16. The erotics of strong curries
17. Cricket
18. Things that aren't cricket
19. Stiff upper lips
20. Rogan josh
21. Things that make you go *gosh!*
22. Past life experiences
23. The difficulty of sending books through the post vis-a-vis sliding the packages through the slits on the Royal Mail boxes
24. Highbrow
25. Lowbrow
26. No brows at all.

Spike told me that he had no brows at all. They'd been singed off permanently in a small house fire that he'd started during one of his hallucinating periods. The tangled white bushy things above his eyes looked real enough to me. But when I threatened to give them a good pull and prove his story wrong, he shook his head and muttered sadly:

Once I had high, magnificently arched brows. People said they were a real feature of my face. And now look at me. Nothing. Nothing left at all!

By the time dessert came around he seemed almost completely drunk, even though the waiter had assured me during one whispered consultation that Spike was mostly drinking ginger beer. Apparently Spike's doctor, an Anglo-Indian called Dr Hydrabad, had enlisted the help of most of Spike's favourite restaurants in cutting down his drinking. He had since discovered, with the covert assistance of some of Spike's most sympathetic head waiters, that years of the hottest rogan josh had so severely burned Spike's palate that now he could hardly tell the difference between the stiffest hard liquor and weak apple cider.

Apparently Spike's drunkenness, the waiter informed me solemnly, was all in his mind.

Did you know, Spike divulged to me between dessert and coffee, *that Groucho Marx and TS Eliot were pen pals?*

No, I didn't, I replied, knowing that, in inimitable Spike fashion, I was about to be relieved of my ignorance.

Now, you'd think, wouldn't you, that Groucho would have been the pursuer in this particular case, genuflecting at the feet of such towering genius. Oh, shake your head if you want, but we're like that. We always think the serious minds are more important than the comic ones. Even most comedians themselves aspire to tragedy. Anyway, to get back to the story, one night they finally did meet. Eliot was over in London to give an important lecture at a university that had just given him an honorary PhD. After dinner, Groucho takes Eliot into his library and prepares to acquit himself well in any literary discussion that might take place. When they get in there, Eliot, with a conspiratorial whisper, says: 'Thank goodness we're alone. Now we can get down to business.' And what do you think happened next? Mmm? Can you guess? Well, all Eliot wanted to talk about was what he said he'd been waiting years to talk about: Animal Crackers *and* Duck Soup. *You see my point?*

As far as I could tell he had more than one, but by then I was getting used to his lateral narratives. So I was happy to just nod my head and let him keep talking while we sipped coffee. I had a sense that he was telling me something important, profound even. But my attention span was short in those days. As he continued I was glancing over his shoulder to where I could see, outside, a little English snow starting to fall.

Me and George Borges used to write, you know.

Who? I swallowed abruptly.

Apparently, he was a fan of the early Goon Shows. *He used to get tapes sent over from friends in London. Evidently, he was somewhat of an Anglophile.*

I didn't have a clue who he was talking about. Naturally I assumed he was raving.

Borges, as in Jorge Luis Borges, the South American writer, who would start with a real event and weave a fantastic invented story from it. So convincingly that his readers couldn't tell where the truth ended and the fantasy began. Like life really. Just like life.

For a second I sensed he was sniping at me for not knowing about Borges and his storytelling techniques. In fact, my father used the same method to draw his audience into his fantastical verbal inventions. He did it for his amusement as much as for ours. Some might have said he liked the sound of his own voice. But I think, rather, he liked the sound of his own imaginings. Just as Spike did. So I knew how to be a good listener to stories that skirted the edges of credibility. And to understand the need for their creation – how they brought pleasure, solace and challenge to their inventors.

But then I realised there were probably other reasons for Spike's impatience. Perhaps he'd reached the age when he expected – or hoped for – less ignorance from those around him. Or perhaps he realised he was running out of time.

Apparently, just as Eliot had written to Groucho, Borges had written to Spike, sending him long, beautifully penned letters about cricket, polo and Robert Louis Stevenson, which were also full of humble requests for packets of English breakfast tea from Selfridges and shortbread biscuits from Harrods.

I drew the line at getting him cotton singlets from Marks & Spencer though. The bugger never sent me a cent for everything I shipped over to Argentina. So I'd be damned if I was going to go underwear shopping for him, no matter how bloody famous he was. Talk about your English eccentrics. He was more English and more eccentric than the worst of them! A bloody good writer though. And you know why?

I knew he'd tell me. All I had to do was sit back for a moment while Spike swallowed the last of his enormous cup of black coffee.

Because no matter how much you analyse him, his stories refuse to be known or be pinned down. Like they reinvent themselves over and over, according to whatever information you've got in your head at the time. I like stories like that. And I like life like that too. I like it when the line between truth and invention is permanently blurred. Sometimes that's the only way I can bear it.

He burped, excused himself, said he was experiencing a caffeine rush and lay down on the floor under the table. I smiled brightly at the waiter, who seemed to understand what was going on. This was Spike's world, after all. Wherever he was he made it so, reinventing himself like a Borges story, from one moment to the next.

Later, after helping him out to the footpath, where we stood in lightly falling snow, he asked me: *Do you think that we come back?*

Come back where? I wanted to reply, tempted to keep playing along with this most playful of men. But I said nothing, only hoisting the collar of my coat up over my ears and rubbing my gloved hands together.

Reincarnation. Death and bloody rebirth. Karma. Karma Sutra. The whole circle-slash-cycle of existence. Yes, indeed. I've come back so many times, yet sometimes I feel I'm having the same experience over and over. Except that each time, someone's saying to me, 'Okay, Spike, old friend. This time you've just got to look a little closer.' Problem is, I always want to look further rather than closer. So they keep sending me back. You know what I mean?

I knew what he meant. In a general sense. In the general sense that I could feel what he meant by the way he said it. But as for *knowing* what he meant, no. His brain, reassembled so many times, seemed beyond my comprehension. Some people, I thought, reduce themselves so they only have to look at easily comprehensible things. Others, like Spike, their brains just expand and expand, because they want to exclude nothing, because they want to experience the hugeness, not the smallness, of life.

Next thing I knew, Spike's red face was right in front of mine. I remember noticing how his capillaries looked like threads woven through the material of his skin.

I don't suppose there's any chance of you coming to work for me?

At any other time I wouldn't have thought twice. But at that moment, outside The Tandoori Traveller with a London winter seeping slowly into my bones, I knew that I was at some sort of crossroads. And not just because Spike and I were standing where the roads to Camden and

Notting Hill crossed and diverged. Besides, I didn't know whether I needed a mentor just then. Or a father figure. Or, I thought, looking at the boyish twinkle in his eyes, a spring–winter romance.

Can I call you? I said.

You can. But you won't, will you? He was smiling into my eyes and I could see he wasn't drunk or crazy or insane. He knew exactly what he was doing and saying. And he had from the moment I'd met him.

You know, he continued, *when you've been alive a long time, it's only your body that gets old. Everything else just gets fresher and fresher. That's the irony of it all. Just when you could really enjoy yourself the most, when your spirit is free and you've got your bloody mojo back again, you look down at your flesh and … well, you realise that to anyone else you just seem old. That's the illusion. That's the utter absurdity of it, you see.*

I did see. I saw in his eyes that in non-physical time he was years younger than I was. That if life was circular and non-linear he was way ahead and way behind all in the same moment. He suddenly picked me up and whirled me around. I grabbed on to my hat with one hand and steadied myself on his shoulder with the other. And then he was laughing and laughing. No, not laughing. He was giggling. Like a kid. Or like they reckon a Buddha giggles. Lightly. As if all the cares in the world would fall onto his shoulders like raindrops, dissipating as soon as they touched anything solid.

And then you see, suddenly your flesh isn't as weak as you think it is either, he said, hardly winded at all, as he put me back on my feet. And then with a bow he was away, walking, no, striding up the street, arms swinging by his side, calling back to me: *Don't worry, we'll stay in touch no matter what you decide to do.*

I wondered if snow was starting to fall again as I saw little white fragments float down to the ground around him. But as I began to run after him, calling out with sudden urgency – *Spike. Spike!* – I saw it wasn't snow, but pieces of the white serviettes he had written on all during dinner, and which he was now systematically shredding as he disappeared around the corner.

I called out again. *Spike! Spike!*

I don't know why I ran so desperately, why my heart was pounding, except that all of a sudden I felt an over-whelming rush of love for him, despite the fact he had forgotten to pay for our dinner.

Spike, Spiiiiike, I yelled. *How can I reach you?*

He had given no indication, during the few hours I'd spent with him, that he was capable of walking as fast as he did. Maybe his entire persona, the whole mad-old-guy bit, was an act, a fantastic coat of armour that made his move-ment through the world a little safer.

I stumbled after him, picking up and stuffing into my pocket the shreds of serviettes he'd left like a trail behind him.

Back at my flat, I found it hard to fathom if the whole thing had been a dream, a fantastic invention of the mind under lamplight. As I laid out the tattered scraps, I could see their tiny words here and there, faded by moisture, and little phrases torn in the middle, out of sequence. I heaped the bits into a pile and stared at them; they seemed to form a pile of hopelessly disconnected things, an impossible puzzle.

Somewhere in London, Spike was laughing at me, and I was determined to get in on the joke.

There were numbers, prepositions, Roman numerals, small verbs and one or two nouns. *Moment* appeared twice. The figure *2* was there, either as part of a list (*1* was included as well) or as a substitute for *to*. Or perhaps *too*. *Contained* appeared in large well-defined letters. The Roman numeral *V* was there, as well as *II* and *CX*. Where they fitted, to this day I still don't know. The word *all* was there, as well as the Italian *tutti*, which I think Spike may have included just to mess with my head.

As I arranged and rearranged the words, I had no idea how many vital clues I'd left lying in the gutter. Maybe it didn't matter. Maybe that was the point. To use just what I had to make whatever sense I could.

Finally, some possibilities presented themselves.

All moment is contained to moment.

This:

All is contained moment to moment.

Or my favourite:

Moment to moment all is contained.

I didn't really know what any of it meant. There were no particular conclusions I could draw. Somewhere in London, Spike was laughing. I don't think he was laughing at me. Or anyone in particular. I think he was just laughing.

Bahut Acha in Bharatpur

Like the travel agent in New Delhi, I'd expected The Birder's Inn in Bharatpur to be no more than a one-star hotel. These had become depressingly familiar on my travels through India, and I knew by heart the grim reality of such places: a sparse room with a dusty fan, a tap with a bucket in the bathroom, a bed with a thin foam mattress, a broken lamp. This time, however, the brochure hadn't lied; the hotel really did offer a 'newly appointed room, off the well-beaten road close to the bird lover's paradise', though it was dark when I arrived from Agra, so I didn't know if the road was well beaten or close to any kind of paradise. But I was charmed and relieved by the attractive freshness of the new rooms at The Birder's Inn, the marble floors, the blue linen curtains and matching bed covers. And especially by the size of the bathroom.

My eyes watered when I saw the deep bathtub, the shiny new faucets, the stand-up shower. After two months in India I could smell my own hair, knew the weirdly acrid scent of the dust and grime that had settled in its thickness, the premature greyness suggested by the layers of mist and smog. The usual hand-held showers never offered enough pressure to properly penetrate my thick curls, so I couldn't ever really wash my hair. For a month I'd relied on surface moisture, perfunctory cleansing and leave-in conditioner. Subsequently, my hair had developed textures that had nothing to do with hair. It hung from my head now like a kind of matting: inorganic, hybrid, with odours and consistencies that changed its colour more than any dye I might have used.

The bath looked new. *Oh dear Lord*, my grandmother would have said. *How the marble gleams!* The showerhead was fixed high to the wall, meaning if I wanted to I could stand under its spray like I was standing in a waterfall. Two plump white towels lay side by side on a bathroom rack.

The whole thing was a vision. For weeks I'd dreamed about lowering my body into a tub of water and washing off the grime that had accumulated on my skin. Even the colour of my eyes had changed, from a green to a muddy grey. There'd be no showering tonight: I intended to luxuriate in a long, hot bath.

On my way downstairs I could see, in front of the lodge, a fire burning. It was surrounded by people holding their palms towards its warmth. The owner called out for me to join them, but I declined – I was hungry after the long drive and kept walking towards the dining room.

The lights went off almost as soon as I reached the corner table in the dining room. This was also something I'd grown used to: the temporary nature of electric power.

The cook called out from the kitchen: *Don't worry, madam. We cook with gas!*

I was too content to be worried. In India I'd become used to things that would have irritated me back home. I liked the way my thoughts formed themselves dreamily in darkness, the way the lights went out unexpectedly all through the day and night. I liked the waiting, the empty quality of time that couldn't be ordered or controlled. It always brought me back to the languid days of childhood, when the slow unfolding of things was both exquisite and excruciating.

The cook called out again. *Don't worry, madam. We have generator.*

The dark lessened my gnawing hunger. I could hear myself breathe. I thought about the bath in my room, how the lack of something in one place intensified an experience that might be ordinary in another. *Oh dear Lord*, I whispered to my grandma's ghost, as I imagined heat on my spine, water softening the muscular ache brought about by hard beds, rickety buses, the incessant bruising crush of skin against skin.

I'll just have some dal, I called out.

Bread, madam?

I wanted bread without oil, cooked in dry heat, like the chapattis I bought in the street. There was something honest about fresh heat. I saw red, orange, a slick of blue rising from the centre of a furnace. Felt the quick sharp burning desire in my stomach.

Tandoori naan, I called back.

Had he heard me?

As I settled into my chair I recalled various facts about Bharatpur listed in the hotel's brochure that the travel agent in Delhi had assured me cheerfully were 'all lies'. The town was on the popular driving route from Delhi to Agra to Jaipur that took just over three days. Indians and foreign tourists came for birdwatching and to find accommodation when all the hotels in Agra were full in high season. Nearby there was a national park and a large number of local artists selling paintings of birds, from tiny studios dotted around the main hotels. Bharatpur, though, had something even more unexpected than bath-tubs, stand-up showers and birds, something that the brochure neglected to mention and that I now discovered in a kind of ecstasy: it had silence. My ears searched out peripheral sounds, listening first for the honks and beeps of the never-ending traffic, the underscore of human voices speaking in multiple tongues, the glorious babble of India. But there was nothing familiar in the surrounding silence.

Or in the soft aloneness I felt suddenly in the dining room of The Birder's Inn.

The lights stuttered back on. A few seconds later my plate of dal arrived with a basket of tandoori bread delivered by the cook – a man in a turban, a Sikh perhaps. The dal was yellow and warm and perfectly arranged in a dish shaped like a boat. It had sailed across a vast distance to arrive at my table, gathering its lentils and spices from faraway lands. I pushed my nose down towards it; it seemed a gentle dal, not too oily, lentils lightly swollen in its juices. The cook waited anxiously at my side. I tried to remember how to say *very good* in Hindi. Another cook, Rahul, from the Sanskriti Foundation in New Delhi, had taught me the word one evening in his kitchen.

Actually, Rahul had taught me three things in Hindi that night:

how to say *how are you?*
how to say *thank you*
how to say *very good*.

They were useful words and phrases to know in a country where most people would ask me in English:

How old are you?
Are you married? and
How many children do you have?

The words for *very good* started with a b and sounded like a dance. Rahul couldn't read or write so I'd only learned to spell it phonetically. But for the moment I couldn't remember a thing Rahul had taught me. I nodded my head and gave the turbaned cook a delighted smile.

Okay, madam? Okay?

I wished he wouldn't bow. I couldn't let him bow to me without bowing back. I was the one, after all, who was receiving his graces, who should be bowing to him.

Where you from, madam?

I bowed my upper body and said: *Australia.*

Ah, Australia. Number one cricket team in the world.

Yes, but India very good too, I reassured him.

Australia: number one. India: number two. You like Sachin Tendulkar?

Not as much as I liked the look of this dal and bread, I thought, wondering why in this land of eternal things I'd had more conversations with Indians about Adam Gilchrist, Ricky Ponting and Shane Warne than I'd had about almost anything else.

I like Sachin and Sourav.

Ah, Ganguly? A very fine cricketer, but a bit, how you say, hoity-toity!

And also VVS Laxman, I enthused.

Who can forget his thrilling knock at Eden Gardens in that memorable series of 2001? A double century in the second innings. Supported by my personal hero, Mr Rahul Dravid. I was very proud to be an Indian that day, madam.

I always liked cricket talk. It seemed to distil centuries of cultural differences into some simple numbers and concepts:

twenty-two players, two twelfth men, three umpires, four consecutive innings. You could hit fours and sixes and not have to run. You could run for twos, threes, fives and score incrementally numbered milestones: half-centuries, centuries, double centuries, triple centuries. You could be not out at stumps. Declare. Retire. Run with a runner. Not run with a runner. Run without a runner. Just run. Appeal. Bowl a yorker. A bouncer. A flipper. A googly. Hit to the boundary and over the top into the crowd. You could stand and field in slips. Hit to silly mid-on, be caught in leg gully, and bat before pad.

I'd met Indians who could recite by heart every score of every innings ever played by Sachin Tendulkar. And by Ricky Ponting as well. Children had been pushed forward to me at gatherings and they would list every wicket ever taken by Shane Warne since he began playing cricket. Hearing the numbers roll effortlessly from the lips of these children was like listening to music, like listening to something spiritual, intuitive, irrational yet utterly logical in its simple and random incantations.

Caught behind 67.

LBW 44.

Stumped Gilchrist off Warne for 32.

Clean bowled for 10.

Out for a duck.

Out for a golden duck.

The cook continued, hovering, as the lights stuttered

and went out again. *It thrills my heart that you love our crick-
eters, because you know, madam, Aussies are the best cricket
team in the world. Second to none.*

Outside, someone began playing a raga on a sitar. Not
brilliantly, but not as clumsily as some westerners I'd heard,
the ones who came to India for six months of lessons with
a sitar master as a way of becoming 'more Indian'. I'd
met many of them along the way, in Delhi, in Rishikesh,
heading to Varanasi or Kolkata, on their search for new
sounds, new scales, new disciplines, and the surrender that
seemed to come with it, entwined in the textures of the raga
scales and their seemingly endless permutations.

Back in Brisbane, a composer who'd performed with
Indians in India had told me more about those permutations: how Indian music did things in threes, unlike
western music, which mostly did things in twos and fours.
How it seemed to be based on three principles:

the principle of doing things in threes

the principle of making things grow

the principle of making them shrink.

He described it further like this:

*They play three things three times that shrink while the
rhythms inside them grow.*

I'd been dazzled by all the talk of numbers and things
growing inside shrinking things. I was intrigued by the
circularity of it, the idea of things that mightn't have
a beginning or an end. I thought of the mandalas from

ancient India, the circles resting inside the squares, or vice versa. And the Christian writers, like Dante, who were obsessed with numbers too, who imagined the divine ordering of the world by creating subsets of numerical symbolism – trinities, holy or otherwise. Indian music was driven by textural rather than linear imperatives, unlike the climactic impulse that propelled the cadences of western music. Did this lack of forward movement, this exploring of intricate detail in repeated things, signify a state of existence beyond 'progress', I wondered, when all possibilities of action had been exhausted and the only way forward was down and inward rather than up and on towards something – a conclusion, a cadence, at least some harmonic change? Was the zero that Indian mathematicians had first notated as a big round empty circle, with a balanced space inside and a vast never-ending space around it, the natural signifier of everything that their country's repeated musical rhythms seemed to embody?

The raga melody stopped abruptly. The musician stumbled a few more times over the scale and then seemed to give up. I felt sympathy for them. I'd stumbled and given up many times too. But things would be different now. That's what I always told myself anyway. Perhaps that was why I returned to places like India. To reacquaint myself not with the physical surroundings but with the feelings I experienced within them. To know that things would be different – that another tiny piece of my spirit had been liberated, like those tiny quarter-notes in an Indian scale, released from a dull melody and falling away to nothing.

Things falling away to nothing.

To the infinity of a zero.

India seemed to promise that.

Surprising India, the tourist brochures told me. *Magical India, Mystical India.*

When people asked me why I travelled to the subcontinent I never knew what to say. Was it the mountains, they asked, the seas, the deserts, the plains? Did I come for the gurus, the saints, the Brahmins, the pandits, or the gods or the goddesses? No. It wasn't the Himalayas, the meditations, or the old intelligence that, as Ralph Waldo Emerson had written, 'in another age and climate had pondered and thus disposed of the same questions which exercise us'. It wasn't even for the music, which I always felt was a mystery that would be impossible to understand in one lifetime. So I didn't know why I came to India. Except that perhaps sometimes I imagined myself like the thing inside the music that shrinks inside the thing that grows. Perhaps while India kept growing in its chaotic, random, relentless way, while the pandits and sages and gurus kept pulling it back to its most ancient traditions, I'd keep shrinking until I was reduced to the mysterious zero entity that India had given to the world and now – in particular, in a dark dining room in Bharatpur – given to me, with all the infinite potential of nothingness contained by that most balanced and beautiful number.

*

Bahut acha.

That was it.

The Hindi for *very good.*

Very very good.

Bahut acha.

A cha cha cha.

Starts with a b and sounds like a dance.

When I first learned the words from Rahul I'd laughed with delight and repeated them over and over, like they were part of the lyric to a nursery rhyme. Rahul had thought I was being childish, as I think he secretly believed most western visitors to his country were. But he laughed along with me, flashing his incandescent smile in the candlelight of his kitchen, as if he had swallowed a mouthful of pearls. Later, I took my violin out and strummed a little song I wrote for him called 'Bahut Acha A Cha Cha Cha'. I sang my song for him. I did a little dance for him. It had been a happy moment in Rahul's kitchen. A light, childish, perfectly empty musical moment.

Bahut acha, I called as I felt my way towards the exit of The Birder's Inn, stumbling like a blind woman through the silence that had descended, like something divine, onto my world.

The dal was bahut acha.

Later, lying in a warm bath surrounded by orange candles, I felt embarrassed by how I'd devoured the dal and bread, as if I were a living example of the phrase my grandma liked to say when we were eating too greedily: *Boy oh boy. You really wolfed that down.*

I wondered what the Hindi word for *wolf* was and if, in the warm kitchen of The Birder's Inn, the cook had turned to his assistant near the shadows of the gas flickering on his big iron oven, below icons of the gods, goddesses and Indian cricket heroes that watched over them while they worked, and said in perfect lilting Hindi: *Oh my God. Those hungry western women! That one was famished. She really wolfed it down. Boy oh boy! She really wolfed it down.*

The Flower Lady of Zhongshan Park

I had recently left a place where spring was blooming, where the perfume of blossoming flowers filled the air. Near my house in West End, an inner-city suburb on the banks of the Brisbane River, there were garden walls and fences covered in jasmine flowers, which carry an especially rich aroma that seems to saturate the air on a warm spring evening.

Even though it was autumn in China, I smelled the same aroma one night as I was walking along the footpath towards the New Space-Time Ruili Hotel, where I was staying, in Zhongshan Park, which was part of the business district of Shanghai. The smell was at once so unexpected and so familiar that I had to stop. I followed the scent and discovered behind a dividing hedge a small Chinese woman standing beside a bicycle adorned with flowers. The larger bouquets were arranged around the seat and frame of the bicycle, while the basket at the front was lined with smaller bunches of jasmine blossoms. At first, the woman thought I would be interested in the larger, more expensive blooms at the back: the long-stemmed lilies, the red and crimson carnations, or the pink and yellow roses. So she laughed with genuine surprise when I leaned forward into the basket at the front of the bicycle, buried my face in the little bunches of jasmine and almost sang out with joy.

She giggled. I laughed as I emerged, my face tingling and bright. She said something in Chinese; I answered in English. I pointed at the jasmine.

Duo shao qian? I asked. *How much?*

Huh? she said, shrugging quizzically.

Duo shao qian?

She laughed again, I suppose at my terrible Chinese pronunciation. She said something. I imagined it was a price. I shook my head and held out my hands to convey: *I don't understand.*

She repeated the same words and held up one finger, then five fingers.

I couldn't tell whether this meant fifty, five or fifteen yuan. I responded by holding up ten and then five fingers.

She nodded, laughing. I said *fifteen.*

She said: *Shi wu! Shi wu!*

I repeated her Chinese with my awful Australian accent.

Shi wu? Shi wu?

She laughed so hard she had to bend over and slap her thigh.

Eventually, after much laughing and shrugging and slapping of thighs, the transaction was complete. I went back to my room and put the jasmine in one of the drinking glasses from the kitchen and placed it on the ledge in front of the window. I would perch on this ledge sometimes at the end of the day and watch the street gradually empty of pedestrians and motorists, until the flashing screen above the Cloud Nine shopping mall was switched off and a stillness that seemed unimaginable in the hectic business of the day settled over this part of the city. That night, as I perched on the ledge near the flowers, their perfume reminded me simultaneously of two places, the street where I lived in Brisbane and the street where I now lived in Shanghai.

I bought flowers every couple of days after that. I still didn't know the name of my flower lady, which was what I called her in emails back home. She didn't know my name either. Perhaps to her I was the flower lady too. And though we communicated mostly through the silent international language of gesture and mime, over a short space of time, in this city full of strangers, she became something constant and familiar.

One Thursday just before 10 pm, I sat on the steps outside Starbucks near her bicycle and watched her as she worked. It was quieter than usual and, despite it still being the National Day holiday week, business was slow. My flower lady wanted me to buy some flowers. But I had two full vases already in my room and the only jasmine she had was an old bunch with drooping stems and falling petals.

I offered her some of my takeaway tea; she offered me the dying flowers. She refused my offer, but I accepted hers. I didn't want to take the flowers for nothing so I gave her a few yuan, which made us both happy.

We were silent as she leaned against her bicycle and I sat on the steps, holding my tea in one hand and the rotting flowers in the other. Again I thought of home. And suddenly I thought of hers too. I didn't know where she came from or how far she'd travelled to arrive here, but sometimes I don't know where I come from either, or even what that word – *home* – really means.

I didn't carry a camera with me when I travelled; I took only my laptop and my instrument, usually a violin. So to remember that moment I began to compose some music that only I could hear on the stringed instrument I kept inside me for occasions such as these. Along with the music, I composed a vision in my mind, as I sometimes did – a virtual video clip, if you like – of my flower lady riding her bicycle up the street towards my house in Brisbane. She was smiling and waving as she cycled past gardens and fences and footpaths dripping with jasmine. Then, to make her more graceful as she cycled up the hill, I visualised her in slow motion. And I suddenly felt so free that I even gave her little wings, as she had given my mind and heart wings here in Shanghai so that they could fly more lightly in this concrete and neon and endlessly active world, through the gift of her rotting flowers.

As she rode I lifted my violin on the corner of my street and played for her the melody of a traditional Chinese folk song called 'Jasmine Flower'. The music swelled as she reached the top of the hill. And lining the streets were my neighbours and friends, my family and my colleagues from Brisbane and here in China and from all over the world, holding up ten fingers, then five, as they sang in honour of the jasmine flowers and the lady who sold them, in the echo of a plaintive Chinese melody: *shi wu, shi wu, shi wu.*

Outside Starbucks, my flower lady noticed that I was smiling and singing to myself. I didn't know what she thought I was doing, whether she worried I was one of those crazy people who smile and sing in the street. She laughed again and hit her hand on her thigh.

I waved goodnight to her and said *thank you* in Chinese, *xie xie*, which in my Australian accent sounded like *share share*. I walked back to the hotel, trailing dead flowers as I went, up the stairs, through the lobby, into the lift, along the corridor and through the doorway of my room, shedding petals on the floor beneath me just as I had to shed the skins of my old dead selves whenever I travelled – so that I could arrive in a new place as vulnerable and open as a child might be in a land of giant and mysterious things.

In my room, a fresh bunch of jasmine was arranged in a glass sitting on the ledge, a fragile silhouette against the window, through which I could see the roads and neon and train lines extending out into the unknown darkness of Shanghai.

As I entered, for a split second it was as if time had stretched through space and a tiny portal had opened up in which I could hear a harmonic whisper resonating: *xie xie, xie xie, xie xie.* It was so persistent I had to stop in my tracks and listen. And as I listened I was overcome with gratitude for that moment and for that sound and for the travel that had brought these words and a music so delicate and quiet I had to stop and breathe deeply if I wanted to hear it whisper *share share, share share – thank you, thank you* – as the scent of jasmine from near and far slowly filled the room.

Singing Love Songs in Kathmandu

The bald man stuttered in broken English as he asked the Nepali manager exactly where the Vipassana retreats were being held that month in Kathmandu. I was in the internet café halfway down Freak Street, the cheap tourist area of the city where I'd come to get my Indian visa renewed. I had been answering emails from friends back home when the connection dropped out. I was sitting in front of the black screen and drumming my fingers on the desk in the haughty way I'd acquired with the unstable subcontinental computers.

The manager couldn't be bothered even trying to respond after the man stammered his question for the fourth time. Instead he turned back to his own work, leaving the traveller stuttering to himself.

I turned to look at him, interested in what kind of person made such a sound. He was brown and slim and his head was shaved. I couldn't pick his accent; I thought at first he must be French. From the back he looked like a man who didn't need to claim his space too strongly or loudly. There was something about the unassuming way he stood with his hands in his pockets as he stuttered that made me think of silence.

I wasn't in the habit of engaging with strangers. After being in India for five months, in that country of a billion people, I had learned to keep my head down and my self to myself. I was always drawn, though, to the vibrations of silence around a person.

The internet was still down. I got up from my computer and stood behind the stammering stranger as I spoke to the manager.

I think he wants to know where the Vipassana meditation retreats are held.

Vipassana? The Nepali man beamed at me, while scowling simultaneously at the stuttering man. A scowling beam, I noted in my inner vocabulary. Or a beaming scowl.

The Buddhist retreat, I told him, granting him one of my completely scowl-free beaming smiles.

I turned to the traveller. *Do you know for sure there is one here?* I asked him. He nodded eagerly.

Yes, there's one in Kathmandu, I told the manager.

Ah … yes … there is, he said, pretending that he hadn't known all along as he took a card from underneath the counter and handed it to me.

Here is the number. And the internet address is dhamma dot org. You can Google it, madam.

I handed the card to the stranger. *There you go.* I turned to walk out the door to buy some curd from a vendor who had just set up on the broken road near the internet café.

Um ... um ... ahh ... he stuttered.

Just ring the number. They'll help you.

I knew the rules of engagement: smile sweetly and keep on moving. Besides, my mouth was watering already at the thought of the curd making its way, soothingly, down my throat.

Could you ...? Would you ... um ... ah ... would you? He smiled again, embarrassed.

Can't you ... um ...? I found myself stuttering like him. I took the card back from him and asked the manager for the phone. I rang the number and waited while it connected. After a few rings I turned and asked the traveller: *Who shall I say the booking is for?*

Um ... um ...

I couldn't wait for him to finish. I just said, *Gabriel.*

Huh?

You're Gabriel, aren't you, I said, more a statement than a question.

He laughed again. *I'm anything you want me to be.*

So? I teased him. I smiled. It felt like a rainbow had come out across my face after a long bitter storm.

Yes. He nodded. *Gavriel.*

He pronounced it the Hebrew way, with a v rather than a b. I figured then he must be one of the thousands of Israelis who travel through India and Nepal every year.

His name wasn't Gabriel; of course it wasn't. Yet from that moment on he would be Gabriel and all that particular name entailed.

I had hardly ever thought of the name before, but I often gave my friends names other than the ones they were assigned at birth. I had changed my own name several times too, and went by Lily in those days. It was like being reborn, I would explain, a chance at a new approach to life. Name-changing was playful and fun, but also significant and, I believed, transforming.

I didn't think about transforming anything, though, when I casually renamed Gabriel. I didn't associate the name with angels, as other people immediately did when I mentioned the name later. It didn't register at all that it had Biblical references, and I would find out only much later that the name was significant in Islam and Judaism as well as Christianity, and even in the New Age book of angel names I would pick up in a crystal shop a few years after I first met my Gabriel in Freak Street. It was just a momentary playful thing, the way I called him Gabriel. I liked the sound of it and the fact that, as well as a man's name, it was also a woman's name, although with a slightly different spelling: Gabrielle. But if there is significance in a name, I would discover later that I had chosen his well.

*

He caught up with me further up the road, where I was spooning my curd out from its unglazed bowl. He glanced at my collarbones and at my shoulders, which were uncovered in a thin-strapped camisole.

You know you really shouldn't walk around like that.

Like what? I answered, feigning innocence.

You should cover yourself up.

Who are you, my father? The question wasn't intended to be rude; I said it with the smile that was starting to feel familiar as it spread across my face again. *Sorry*, I said immediately, licking the sweet curd off my spoon. *Sorry.*

No ... I'm not your father. But women who don't cover up get themselves into a lot of trouble in ... in ... in ... in ... in ...

I spooned the curd into my mouth as I waited while his stutter worked itself out in his brain then his mouth.

... in India.

I know about the dress code there, I replied cheekily. *I've been covering up there for five months. I thought Nepal was different. I mean, it's Kathmandu!*

It *was* different here in Kathmandu. We were standing in Freak Street after all, the street made famous by the hippies and stoners who arrived in the '70s, when it was possible for a dropout from the west to live on dope, hash and Nepali food for years without ever having to go home.

Some of them had never left; the street was still full of freaks. They gathered down the road at the Snowcap Café,

43

just the Snowcap to locals, or 'the Snow, man' to the hard drug users, eating fresh cakes and pies just like the travellers who'd journeyed overland through Europe and the Middle East in the '60s and '70s. Marijuana was freely available then in Nepal and you could still see the consequences of this largesse in the psychedelic paintings that hung on the café's walls. They were faded and covered in layers of grime now, much like the ageing western junkies and hippies who'd had their peak years back in the '70s. Some of them still hung around Freak Street hoping to reclaim those times by holding court with the young travellers. To these modern kids, the shared joints and hookahs on the foot-path outside the Snowcap were part of a much safer rite of passage, and you could tell by their motorbikes and iPods that the trek to Nepal had been a whole lot easier for them; that they had mostly bypassed countries like Iran, Iraq and Syria, through which relatively safe travel was still possible 'back in the day'.

I didn't particularly like the Snowcap. It had that smell of decay and worn-out brains that I found depressing in a country as impoverished as Nepal. There always seemed something unseemly about dropouts in a place where the roads were never properly paved and where most of the young people listened to western pop, loved rock'n'roll and would've given anything for a good pair of designer jeans – where the dream was to drop in rather than out. I had done the manda-tory thing the day I first arrived in Freak Street, though, and strolled over to the Snowcap to eat some freshly baked apple pie and sip a glass of Nepali tea and watch the tribes of travellers stroll up and down the street.

The place seemed quieter now. The locals had probably realised there was more money to be made from the affluent tourists, especially the mountain climbers, for whom the more fashionable Thamel area, with its gift stores and music shops pumping out the latest CDs onto the crowded street, had become too pricey. They had started to come to this part of old Kathmandu to rest in one of the cheap but clean lodges, engage their sherpas in Durbar Square and wait for the climb upwards to begin.

I vaguely recalled seeing Gabriel the night I arrived at the Annapurna Guest House, remembering how I had averted my eyes, as I had learned to, from his gaze. Now I accepted his gaze fully for the first time as I tugged my top up a little. I knew what he meant. The decorum of travel, I called it. It struck you in the strangest places and you found yourself saying the most unexpected things, like the time in Rishikesh when I had primly lectured a young Australian girl on wearing a bra to cover her cleavage and not wearing shorts so short you could see her bottom. I might have dressed like this back home, at the beach, for example, but I felt it impolite, and even a bit dangerous, to do so in India. Travelling surprised me in ways that even I found surprising. I became prim where once I was open-minded, free where I might have felt more cautious.

Can ... can ... can I show you something really beautiful?
Gabriel suddenly asked me.

I had heard that line before, but not stuttered. The stutter made it seem more intriguing than it might have normally.

Okay, I said, shrugging, as I spooned out the last of the curd from its brown bowl.

It's just this way ... He held out his arm and pointed up Freak Street towards Durbar Square.

You're not going to take me to that temple full of monkeys, are you? I asked, now suspicious. A Nepali man had offered to show me this for a fee the day I had first arrived in Kathmandu.

Oh, no ... though that is very interesting and beautiful too.

He had stopped stuttering: it came like a break in a storm. I wondered vaguely about this anomaly, about the things that made a man stutter and stumble and the things that didn't.

Then what? I asked. *Where?*

Come with me and I'll show you. He turned to go, noticed I hadn't moved and turned back to me, held out his hand and smiled. *Come.*

He said it so simply and matter-of-factly. It wasn't an order; it was an invitation. I didn't take his offered hand. I was too cautious, too independent for that. But I followed him the same way he had invited me – simply and matter-of-factly, as if it was something I always did.

Those who knew me well knew I didn't follow easily. I thought about this as I walked, slightly behind him, picking my way around the potholes and breakages, past the Snowcap Café, and up along the road that led away from Freak Street into the congested heart of Kathmandu.

I can't remember where we walked: even if I had a map, I would never be able to retrace the route we took that day. I know we were lost several times, walking down alleyways in the back lanes of Kathmandu, emerging into squares teeming with bicycles and rickshaws, or market-places where rows of brightly clothed Nepali women sold fresh chillies, dried beans and piles of pomegranates. I also remember we passed outdoor butchers selling slabs of meat, cured orange and covered in flies, and rotting carcasses hanging on hooks.

If it had been anyone else I would have been too impa-tient to keep following him. Once or twice I got angry with Gabriel as he stood at yet another intersection trying to figure out where to go. He didn't exactly scratch his head, in that clichéd signal to mean he was lost. But he did look right and left, forwards and backwards, again and again. I guess I stuck with him because of his easy physical energy, the slow way he ambled through the crowds, the amusing confidence with which he guided me this way – *down here* – and that.

His philosophy right from the beginning seemed to be *it doesn't matter how long it takes as long as you enjoy the journey to get there.* Since arriving in India five months before, I'd heard enough people say that to be sick of how trite it sounded. But from Gabriel, with whom the journey was enjoyable, even though it was so full of flaws, failures, backtracking and circling, it seemed refreshingly original and completely true.

We stopped at one of the marketplaces that seemed to spring up around every corner. Gabriel insisted on buying me something to eat, a pastry so thick with glassy sugar that it shone. I could feel the will beneath his casual ease and felt cautious about putting myself in his hands, but this feeling soon passed in the excitement of the encounter and the stimulation of our expedition into the heart of old Kathmandu.

We sat on two old crates as we ate, tearing the pastry into strips and sharing them between us. As we did, a Nepali man approached us and began to talk to me.

I have the money to take you anywhere you want to go, he said, surprising us both with his audacity. He seemed a humble man, slightly desperate in his loose white shirt and too-long flared pants.

I have saved money for ten years hoping to meet a great lady like you, he told me, bowing slightly as he spoke.

Gabriel winked at me.

If he can afford to take you places I can't, perhaps you should go with him, he said, amused rather than irritated by my suitor.

I think it was my floppy black hat, which I had bought the day I arrived in an overcast yet sultry Kathmandu, that made me seem more sophisticated than I was. I wasn't nearly as beautiful as the most ordinary Nepali or Indian woman, but my pale skin and green eyes made me exotic to the locals.

Made bolder by my friendly smiles, the Nepali man pulled up a seat right next to mine.

Gabriel stood up, laughing, and said: *Wait here if you like.*

Hey, I called out as he walked away. *Weren't you going to show me something beautiful?*

Wait here and I'll bring it to you, he called back. *I'm not going to compete for you. I'll be back when you're free.*

I'm free now. And I don't know how to get back.

I can show you the way, my new companion said. *Where are you staying?*

Freak Street, I told him, perturbed by Gabriel's abrupt departure. The man didn't recognise the western name.

Near Durbar Square, I added. I felt too sorry for him to get up and walk away myself, so I let him buy me a tea and offer his services to me. He was already planning our trip in his new car to the Kathmandu Valley when Gabriel returned, smiling. He was holding an envelope of photographs in his hands.

Here it is, he said, ignoring the Nepali man.

Where is what? I asked, now a little haughty.

He waved the photographs in front of my face. *Something really beautiful.*

I wasn't surprised. Or deflated. Not by the photographs anyway. I was surprised that I was so interested in them and also that I didn't feel deflated at all that he had led me all this way to show me some holiday snaps.

He stood silently as he waited for his rival to take off.

Um … ah … I stammered in the broken language I had recently picked up from Gabriel. *Sorry,* I managed to say to the Nepali man, whose name I realised I had not even bothered to ask, *that's not going to work out for me.*

This man is your husband? he asked mournfully.

Oh no, I told him, laughing just like Gabriel was laughing. *We only just met.*

Gabriel pulled up a chair and sat down close to me, not even bothering to pretend for the sake of the sad-eyed Nepali that he hadn't won their contest for my attention.

Good luck, I said to my conquered suitor. *You should still take that trip.*

A man like this is not good enough for a great lady like you, he said unexpectedly.

I looked up at him, stricken as he was stricken by his outburst.

This Israeli … I've seen them come here for years.

How can you tell? I asked him, suddenly oblivious to Gabriel next to me. *I mean, how can you tell he's from Israel?*

He's ugly enough to be a Jew, he whispered to me.

Gabriel laughed again. I felt defensive.

I'm sorry, I said coldly to the Nepali. *I can't help you but I wish you luck*.

He withdrew, stumbling into the crowds of shoppers as I watched. I felt ill, as if someone had told my fortune and I hadn't liked what they had seen.

Gabriel shrugged. *Don't worry about it. We have problems like this all the time.*

It doesn't bother you?

Not any problem, he said. *Now let me show you something beautiful … just like I promised you.*

It was difficult to understand what had just happened. What was happening at that moment and what was going to happen.

Come on, he repeated encouragingly. *It's really not any problem. Not for you anyway. Look at you. Like he said, you are an angel. But I can show you somewhere beautiful that I have been. Here* – he held out his hand towards me again; this time it held the envelope of photographs. *Let me show you.*

There were snow-capped mountains and skies as blue as the sea. There were clouds in shapes I had never seen and faces of brown-skinned women radiant in the high altitude. There were goats and sheep and pictures of tiny flowers almost crushed under a climbing boot. There were shots of young Nepali boys hauling white bags on their backs and children walking barefoot on icy stones. And there was Gabriel with the peaks of Mount Everest in the background, his arms raised either side of him as if he were embracing the whole world, his long brown face distorted into a kind of smiling ecstasy.

Everest base camp, he stammered to me as I examined the photos one by one. When I had turned all of them over I pushed them into a little pile and looked at them again. *They always say the mountain can change your life.*

Roland Barthes, one of my favourite writers, calls a photograph a text. There are ways of reading a photograph the same way you would a poem or a book. You can also read photographs as the story of the photographer: the person who chooses those specific moments, those images and those faces on which to settle his or her attention. All of their decisions matter in the story the image will tell: the route they take in their travels, the sidesteps, the pauses, the stumbles and the falls, every minute contingency of their lives that leads them to arrive at that exact moment when the photograph is there, perfectly composed, ready to be taken. A minute later or earlier and the photograph, and the story it tells, would be altered irrevocably.

To follow the view of the photographer, some say, is to follow their mind and their heart and, for those who believe in it, their soul. Gabriel's photographs conversed with me in ways he couldn't verbally. And as I looked, I could hear a little of the man that he had been and perhaps would become.

His photographs told me the story of a man who had

been reborn from climbing up the foothills of a high mountain. They told me of someone who saw beauty in the smallest thing, even the pats of cow dung with which the Nepalis insulated their huts in the cold – Gabriel had photographed these with the same reverence he might have had for the beauty of a young woman. There were also shots of the gnarled face of an old woman looking up pensively into the eye of the camera, her back made crooked by the years she had carried burdens up and down the Himalayan slopes. Underneath this face in the pile of images was a picture of an old man with eyes buried deep inside folds of skin, peering intently as if he knew the stories hidden inside those black slits would forever tantalise the viewers of a photograph that might travel miles and miles around the world – but only those who had lived his hard cold years of toil could ever know his secrets. He tantalised me then, as I sat beside Gabriel, and I felt a little of what explorers into unknown terrains must have felt when they came across things they had never seen or even heard about: the shock of recognition, awestruck by the strange and unfamiliar.

Even if I couldn't read between the lines of all the stories these photographs told, Gabriel's stuttered comments in his broken English filled in subtexts.

So beauty … he would mutter, shaking his head in wonder. *So beauty.*

I didn't want to correct his faulty grammar. Or adjust his wonky syntax. I didn't even want to turn to look at him. I just wanted to stare at the photos, and study them as I might the images of the great painters of the world, because I felt his reverence too, felt how his eye must have taken in all the details of the world around him as he lifted the camera and clicked; it filled my body with wonderment.

Wonderment: I had loved this word as a child. I remembered the moment I had first heard it. As soon as I could, I had run to my father's library underneath the house and found his copy of *Roget's Thesaurus*. In the dusty pages of what would become a dog-eared paperback covered in stains and grubby fingerprints, I found wonderment and other delectable words such as *astonishment, surprise, bewilderment, stupefaction*. All these words might one day, I hoped, lead me somewhere truly mysterious and undiscovered.

It had come upon me unexpectedly, this wonderment. It only lasted a few moments and then I was the same adventurous but fundamentally cautious traveller I had been before I met Gabriel two hours ago. But during those moments I could see and feel what he saw and felt: the beauty of the simple faces, the tenderness of the tiny alpine flower wavering between ragged rocks, the almost surreal formation of clouds through which the distant peaks jutted. And there and then I wanted to know what had led him to see things the way he did. To know the story behind his long brown face smiling at the camera. And his eyes and the history of their gaze.

He leaned close to me as he spoke.

I did it, you know. It is unbelievable to think. Two years ago I was a fat sick man. I turned fifty and decided to climb the mountain and there I am.

And there he was. It was a simple fact. Indisputable. There was the photographic evidence on the grimy table in front of me. But I understood as I looked at a picture of him standing at the top of a low peak, a picture that somehow had stuck to the bottom of the pile so that it had to be peeled away from another photograph in order to be seen, that it must have taken him thousands and thousands of steps to get there.

We were quiet as we began our walk back to Freak Street. Neither of us had a clue where we were going, or how we would find our way back to our hotel. But neither of us seemed to care. As we walked, we spoke a little, exchanging details about our lives. He told me he lived half the year in Haifa in Israel and the other half 'in the east'. The names of the places where he had travelled seemed to roll off his tongue with little effort. I was beginning to recognise a pattern in what caused his voice to tremble and what didn't.

I noticed he rarely stuttered when he spoke about his travels. Perhaps for his mind there was freedom in the names of the places in Asia he had been: India, Thailand, Laos, Vietnam, Cambodia; everywhere except Malaysia and Indonesia, two countries denied to him as an Israeli citizen. The names sounded like music when he said them.

Not because of his voice but, in a similar way to how I had felt seeing his photographs, because I could feel the magic in the list of his destinations – I didn't just want to travel to those places myself, but, even more mysteriously, I felt I had already been there.

In return, I told him about the songs I had been writing in India. These were songs that I sang accompanying myself, strumming my violin like a ukulele. *Some people take photographs of their travels*, I explained. *I make songs.* I thought that Gabriel, having taken those shots in the mountains, would understand how a song could be composed out of being in a place, just as a photograph could.

He didn't seem that interested, but I was beginning to realise that Gabriel sometimes kept his immediate response to things well hidden, almost as if he needed to ingest words, turn them over and examine them deep inside him before he could make sense of them and then respond. As we walked further on, he asked me three questions.

How do you record them?

Are they for a CD or just for your own use?

How do you write a song?

I had a MiniDisc player that I used to collect sounds from my travels. But its quality wasn't good enough to record my songs. And, in any case, it was difficult to record myself. I was looking for a recording studio, I told him – somewhere in India, I imagined, where I was headed after I got my new Indian visa, which I had come to Kathmandu to obtain. Or perhaps in Paris, where I would go after India's temperatures became too unbearable, before the notorious monsoons began in July.

Gabriel told me he loved music and that his latest obsession was Leonard Cohen. You could get a lot of cheap CDs in Kathmandu, and Cohen's back catalogue featured prominently in most of the little CD shops around Freak Street and Thamel. I was a fan too, but not obsessed the way Gabriel seemed to be. I imagined that if Gabriel could sing he might sing like Leonard Cohen, a deep, sometimes twisted growl carved out from his body.

I was used to these segues in conversations about music when I brought up my own songwriting, used to how the subject of my songs often involved people making conversational detours into discussions of artists they already knew and loved. It had been a long time since this bothered me. I knew that people needed to relate to things, how new things often had to be understood in terms of old familiar things. And it would be hard, anyway, to explain without sounding like a crazy person how sometimes new songs seemed to drop onto my body like tiny fragile creatures from the sky; how at first they seemed, even to me, alien and new; how they needed patience and careful tending and sometimes extended periods of privacy and silence so my relationship with them could grow. How getting to know and understand a newly created song by singing it over and over until everyone around you was driven mad by the repetition was a process that could feel like falling in love. How taking the song into your body could be akin to taking into your flesh the shape and form of a lover; how you needed to breathe carefully and deeply in order to find the rhythm of a new song, as you would the rhythms of a new lover; how you needed to be close while still distant; how you needed to merge, yet still observe.

After an outpouring of new songs during my months in India, Kathmandu had seemed at first like a hiatus, a pause in my musical adventures. But already I had written two new songs in my hotel room, and I began each day in a ritual of song the way a religious person might begin their day in prayer. It centred me and made me feel connected. Sometimes a song was the only anchor in a traveller's world full of change and movement. Song helped me to acknowledge what I had loved, what I had left behind and what I might love in my new environment.

I tried to tell Gabriel some of these things as we walked. Sometimes, if there was nothing to say, he would wander ahead of me looking this way and that, like an animal trying to find its way home. It wasn't easy to get a sense of where we were in relation to where we had been or even where we were going. Kathmandu offered these discombobulations even more than hectic New Delhi did in India. The streets and alleys that were packed with human and animal traffic as we crisscrossed the city had a strangely dismantling sense of disorder, as if structures of thought and sense perceptions could crumble with each step we took. I contemplated what effect the city and its squalid dreaming must have had on the stoners of the '70s, wandering the cities in their colourful, woven-cotton uniforms of striped, flared drawstring pants and vivid T-shirts, their long dreadlocks flicking flies out of their faces as they made their way through the maze of lights. I felt out of it while completely sober. But perhaps being out of it in Kathmandu might allow one to make more sense of everything.

The sky was dimming, so the lights of the bazaars and stores and the headlights of the motorbikes that roared through the crowd gave our surroundings a fantastical sheen. The people around us were mostly locals, but occasionally our paths would intersect with those of other travellers: young backpackers smiling broadly in the noisy chaos; or the mountain climbers from Britain or Northern Europe, stomping through the crowds in their thick-soled boots, looking like pale-skinned giants.

Gabriel suddenly spoke after one of our long silences.

On top of the world, he stammered.

Huh? I offered back, amused yet puzzled.

It really has the feeling, don't you think, as if we are at the top of the world.

For some reason the song of the same name by The Carpenters started playing in my head. *Stop it*, I whispered to myself. I should be hearing something different in this place that travellers from all over the globe have called the top of the world, a tapestry of Hindu and Buddhist texts perhaps, laid over droning ragas and mantras, with a hint of techno doof to reference the encroaching technological age of the subcontinent.

The phrase was appropriate though. On top of the world. It resonated with dreams of climbers and travellers to high places. I wondered how far the phrase could be traced back through time, imagining, for instance, the shock of the words in the vocabulary of a world still believed to be flat.

I liked to imagine what explorers must have first felt like when they came upon mountains whose peaks they could not see. Further to the west, the Pamir Mountains had been called 'the roof of the world' by travellers who first sighted them. It had always delighted me, this image of a roof, as if the earth were a house whose layers and storeys were enclosed by a thick canopy of mist and snow.

How else could early travellers make sense of what they had seen except to fashion metaphors that related to the humble things they knew – to roofs and houses? Or the metaphor of opposites that defined their consciousness of the world and its limits – tops and bottoms, heaven and hell, good and evil, gods and angry demons? They might also have had to invent words to describe new and unfamiliar feelings: it was thrilling to imagine that sense of expanding towards language adequate to encapsulate experience, groping around in the dark for the means to communicate to another the precise nature of a thought, feeling or response. The effort it must have needed – as intense as the physical strength needed to carve a space for living out of the wilderness – to carve out words.

For fleeting seconds along the roads of Kathmandu I felt I might have physically arrived at that place where I once dreamed words might take me. And that a man who didn't know many English words, who probably couldn't spell the ones he could pronounce and who mangled the few he did know, was leading me there.

Everything I knew was turning upside down. Upside down at the top of the world. Would that make me right side up at the bottom of the world? I didn't need drugs to blow my mind. That was the gift of travelling, of covering any distance by foot, by machine or with the mind – that sense of following a person, a dream, the footsteps of others, or an idea or concept through the wilderness, until at its pure, distilled centre you could find something with which to light the way a little further through the next wild territory.

Around a corner we passed a Nepali man clothed in white and carrying a young girl on his shoulders. The child was dressed in magenta so shiny it threw off rays of rainbow colours all around the pair, making them look as if they were travelling through a kaleidoscope. As they walked, he was pointing things out along the road in what sounded like Nepali, and she squealed with delight every time he spoke. Sometimes he squealed back. In reply she sang. Then he did. Once or twice they sang together, the interweaving voices a beautiful duet. I slowed down so they could overtake me, almost embarrassed at my greed, my delight in the child's delight. It should have been enough that I let the intersection between the father and daughter and me and Gabriel be as fleeting as it was meant to be.

I thought of my own father then. He was a great reader of books but even he was driven nuts by the questions I asked in my attempt to find connections between all manner of things: history and language, art and science, the past and the present. *Don't think about things so much*, he would advise me. *Accept more and question less.*

Perhaps this is what he meant, I thought, not to grasp too much or too hard, to be happy with tiny moments. To let them pass by you with little remark. But I felt moved to observe and also to celebrate, to honour the relationship between a father and a curious daughter halfway across the world from where my father had tried to guide his own curious daughter, although I couldn't remember being hoisted, literally, on my father's shoulders. It always moved me to see fathers and daughters sharing joy in a discovery, the simple homage of the father in lifting the girl onto his shoulder.

I remembered a conversation I had with my father when I was about ten and I had first begun my restless quest to make sense of history – of the inexplicable leaps that progress seemed to make. Even though I couldn't articulate exactly what unsettled me, I had a sense that I wasn't being told the whole story. One day, I thought, I will have to explore the world to discover such things, but for the moment I relied on the journeys my father and I made, along with my sisters and brothers, to the Toowong library, where the books of the world I hoped to one day traverse were kept.

We were in the car on our way back home from one of these regular trips. In my lap I had my usual pile of books about seemingly disparate subjects: pirates, the history of the English monarchy, silent cinema and the history of fashion, along with Georgette Heyer detective stories and plays by Tennessee Williams and Edward Albee. Dad mentioned to me that one day there would be more discovered than undiscovered things. The thought of this not only baffled me but made me sad. What would a person do, I wondered, if there were no more things to find out?

It was moving to think how a human being could be humbled by the grandeur and magnificence of what they had discovered. I craved such experience, of feeling small, dwarfed by mystery, humbled by what I was yet to know. Was that sense of awe essential to survival, I wondered? Did the fragility of unknowing bring some necessary caution and tenderness to my life – that sense of feeling one's way, dumbly, towards a mystery?

But whatever romance a traveller might have about peak experiences at the top of the world, the reality of Kathmandu required a less poetic approach. It didn't help at all to raise your eyes to the skies or dream of ascending. To make your way across the metropolis you needed to direct your eyes downwards, if only to avoid the piles of cow dung that decorated the footpath, the honking bikes and their mad drivers, as well as the piles of spit and phlegm that the locals hacked with rhythmic regularity on the ground in front of them. Even during the few days I had been in Kathmandu I could tell how hard it might also be to maintain your spirits in the poverty that lay beneath the exotic otherness of the city. If travelling had taught me anything, it was not to romanticise places. From the privilege of my hotel rooms it was possible to believe in any fantasy, but for the locals, without these freedoms, reality was a different story altogether.

For the moment, though, I was too occupied with finding the route back to Durbar Square to enjoy the exhilaration of metaphor that had recently lifted my spirits and opened my heart towards the man I was still following through the darkening streets.

And then all of a sudden we were in front of a side street that appeared to lead to another little square I didn't recognise from our earlier route. Gabriel was sure we had passed it, though, on our way in from Durbar Square.

Come this way, he told me, even though my instincts told me to keep walking straight.

Why? I was growing weary and suspicious now that we might be taking another wrong turn.

Just come, he insisted.

Where are we? I asked petulantly.

How do I know?

Well, have you been here before?

He was amused, but sanguine. *Of course not. But come with me anyway.*

It was because I'd seen his photographs that I had begun to trust his instincts. My faith in his judgement had no logical foundation, but I had seen the beauty he had observed, and I wanted to share in the possibility he seemed to perceive in the most unpromising things. Perhaps something beautiful lay ahead of us – perhaps in the square. Perhaps it would be nothing. But I was curious to see what exactly it could be.

To get to the square, which seemed to enclose another square inside its perimeter, we had to step around the potholes piled with rotting vegetables, rubbish and old rancid food. We pressed on through the stench, making our way through the groups of young men with imitation leather jackets who sat around smoking and chatting in Nepali, oblivious to any new strangers in their midst.

Close to the entrance of the square I could glimpse inside: prayer flags were fluttering in the city's amber twilight. As we walked through the entrance we could see the Buddhist stupa in the centre of the square, and behind it a temple doorway through which shaven-headed monks were entering and leaving. Other monks sat under the stupa quietly praying or chatting happily. To the left of the square's entrance, a small café with red and white chequered tablecloths promised authentic noodles and dishes as well as 'specials for foreigners'.

Gabriel and I stopped close to the stupa. We said nothing as we looked around in wonder at what we had stumbled upon.

So beauty, Gabriel whispered. *So beauty.*

What is this place? I asked, although Gabriel knew as little as I did about what it was or even how we had got there. *Some kind of temple?* I couldn't recall seeing any mention of this square, or this temple, in any of the tourist sites about the wonders of Kathmandu.

Monks wearing saffron and scarlet robes continued to silently file through the entrance, and from inside we could hear echoes of the low chanting that was known throughout the west as the soundtrack of Tibetan Buddhism, the deep throaty *om* that seemed to carry within it centuries of history, both territorial and spiritual.

We sat for a while and listened. I closed my eyes and breathed in the smells of the approaching night, the scent of curries, of noodles being fried and boiled, along with the unrelenting fumes of motorbikes and cars and all the small fires that burned along the routes we had walked that day, leaving a haze of ash and embers like a smoky veil across the city.

I suddenly felt tired and wished that I was confident of how to get back to the hotel on my own. Gabriel could sense my restlessness. He cleared his throat and began to stammer.

Maybe this is a good place for you to come and sit. For your music, I mean. Just listening could inspire you.

I just want to go back to the hotel, I said. I could write a song there in peace and quiet.

Are you hungry? We could eat before we go.

No, I said impatiently. *I'd like to go back now.*

We fell back into silence again and listened further to the chanting. There was something mesmerising in the open throats of the monks, the oscillation of soundwaves and resonance. I could feel it calming both of us down and making us easier with each other.

After a few moments, I got up and began to walk alone around the square. Next to the temple was a little clothes shop selling Tibetan artefacts. Beside it was a stall selling electronic equipment. And then, the most unexpected thing. In the furthest corner of the square I saw a sign above the entrance to a laneway. *STUDIO ACOUSTICA*, it announced in black cursive letters. *For all your recording needs.* The words were accompanied by a drawing of a small lotus flower. I thought I must have been dreaming it.

See, you have found what you were looking for, I heard Gabriel say as he walked up behind me. *Every day is a miracle.*

Wonder what kind of studio it is, I mused. *It couldn't be a recording studio. In here, in the middle of the temple square.*

Gabriel walked around me and headed into the laneway. As I followed him I remembered something I'd read once about the angel Gabriel, that he was the guardian of the gates of paradise, as well as a protector of musicians.

I didn't believe in heaven or hell, not in a religious sense anyway. But in the middle of a dirty city where monks were chanting in the hope of nirvana themselves, we had stumbled upon a place to record my songs, high up here at the top of the world. And Gabriel, whom I would one day call my Gabriel, had led me there.

The grind of electric guitars, badly played, echoed from inside the studio. There could not have been more of a contrast with the chanting monks outside. I heard a blues riff, then a familiar rock'n'roll anthem, before a tall, good-looking young Nepali man walked out from a room and stood in front of us. I thought he must be a music student. Or possibly one of the creators of the rudimentary riffs we had heard.

He smiled nervously and wiped his hands on his jeans, which looked brand new.

Can I help you? he asked.

I held my hand out, formally, as if to signal that I took him seriously.

You work here? I said, as Gabriel looked around.

Yes, he replied shyly. *I'm the manager. Welcome to Studio Acoustica.*

He couldn't have been more than eighteen. Back home in Australia he would have still been a gangly boy, probably going to university or living at home with his parents. Here the boy was a man in charge.

I shook his hand. *Hi, I'm Lily. This is Gabriel.*

My name is Bizou, madam. Sir. Are you French, Lily?

Why do you ask if I'm French?

I thought you might be.

No. But I know bisous means 'kisses' in French.

I had embarrassed him. And myself. I could feel Gabriel's smile warming me from behind. We all paused, realigning ourselves to the new parameters of our interaction. I wondered how many other westerners had wandered into Bizou's studio.

You have recording facilities here? I asked him. *For acoustic instruments?*

That's our specialty. Come. He gestured down the corridor. *I'll show you.*

He led us down the narrow passage into a side room

where a twenty-four-track desk was set up in front of a glass partition. I could smell not only the fresh paint of the room but the effort and ambition it must have taken to set it up.

I only need a few tracks, I told Bizou. *I have some songs I would like to lay down. Just simple things.*

He nodded, eagerly. I enjoyed his immediate enthusiasm.

If you need other musicians, we can provide that too, he offered.

Gabriel was still nosing his way around the facilities. He had walked behind Bizou and me, unobtrusive yet present in the discussion as we all walked into the main part of the facilities. I had been in numerous studios around the world, and I could sense the care that had gone into setting up Studio Acoustica.

You did all this yourself? I asked Bizou.

I'm not the owner. That's Jack. He imported the desk and the microphones from America. They're state of the art.

He said it with such simple pride that I felt overwhelmed with emotion. Kathmandu was such an impoverished place, but here in this clean, newly equipped studio, one could sense how young Nepalis like Bizou reached out into the world.

That's fantastic, I said encouragingly, wondering at the same time whether I sounded condescending. I was surprised more than anything else. And delighted.

I was also curious, though, at the proximity of the studio – and its technology and western-inspired rock'n'roll – to the vibrations of the monks.

How did you end up here? I asked.

Bizou scratched his head, trying to find the right words to explain.

It was the cheapest place available in the area. We also think it brings us good luck. And so far it has.

I turned to Gabriel, who was standing behind us, discreetly allowing me to make my arrangements in private. *Perhaps it will bring me luck too.*

Someone down the corridor was starting up a grungy riff again. It sounded like AC/DC's 'It's a Long Way to the Top (If You Wanna Rock'n'Roll)'. In the spaces between the out-of-tune chords, I thought I could make out the drone of the monks emanating into the studio. It made for a strangely poignant tapestry of sound. We listened for a while until even Bizou looked pained.

We love our rock'n'roll in Nepal. And our blues, he explained with a kindness that would have seemed impressive even from a much more mature person. I gestured in the direction of what I could only – even euphemistically – call a cacophony.

We rent out the back room as a rehearsal studio, he continued. *Most of the kids here don't have the money to pay much. But like everywhere else in the world there's always someone dreaming of being a rock star.*

I was impressed again at how articulate and compassionate he was in depicting the music scene of Kathmandu.

Nepal is a very poor country but we love American music. Not just rock'n'roll bands. Songwriters too. We love our singer-songwriters, like Norah Jones and Jack Johnson.

The Js, I joked.

Bizou laughed. *Yes, we love them.*

It was true. That summer in Kathmandu every second shop had Norah Jones or Jack Johnson playing from their loudspeakers. In contrast, I'd never heard their music, or anything that sounded like them, in India. In Paharganj, for instance, the backpacker area of New Delhi, Bollywood music blasted out day and night. You rarely heard anything western in India and the idea of a solo singer-songwriter writing about her personal experience as she moves through the world would have seemed almost infantile there, in a land of one billion people struggling to find formations that made them unified rather than individual and separate. But it was obvious that the Nepalis were at great pains to differentiate themselves as much as they could from their southern neighbours.

I felt in some ways that I was, even temporarily, at home in Studio Acoustica. I was certain I had found a place to record. Gabriel and I briefly discussed timetables, but it was up to me to decide what days I would book in. Bizou and I ambled back into the sound booth and looked through the booking sheets.

There was time available in just under a week, during the last two days before I was due to fly out of Kathmandu. It seemed clear that I should lock in a booking as quickly as possible – it was now or never, as my grandmother might have said. But as usual, when it came to recording my songs, I procrastinated. I never felt I was ready. Never felt I was good enough. My voice needed more work, more strength, more power; it wasn't acceptable the way it was.

Gabriel appeared behind us, encouraging me to make a firm commitment.

He didn't stammer at all as he spoke quietly to me. *Perfect, don't you think, Lily? Just perfect.*

I realised with a shiver that it was the first time I had heard him say my name. Lily. In his deep hesitant English it sounded as gentle as the caress of a flower. I felt ashamed that I had never formally introduced myself to him, that he had found out my name only when I introduced myself to Bizou. Considering how significant names were for me, and that I had been boldly calling him a name of my choosing since we first met, it was strange that I had overlooked mentioning my own name to Gabriel.

It was a day of such strangeness. But at least we were now formally introduced. Gabriel and Lily. Lily and Gabriel. At the top of the world.

I didn't overthink my reply, as I had many things in my life.

Okay. Bizou. I held out my hand to seal the deal. *Yes. Let's go for it.*

I arranged the times and also the loan of Bizou's guitar. He was puzzled when I said I strummed most of my accompaniment on the violin, but I had grown used to such initial confusion. We said our goodbyes to Bizou. As we walked out of the studio into the blue-black night, Gabriel turned to me and, without saying a word, smiled at me in such a way that I could tell he felt wonderment, the same wonderment I had felt when he showed me his photographs, the wonderment that made me recall the wonderment I first felt as a child. And I knew then that perhaps I was about to introduce him to something beautiful and surprising too.

The walk back to our hotel was like a dream. After the serendipity of our discovery in the Tibetan square, Kathmandu seemed carnivalish. The brightly coloured saris that adorned the Nepali women and girls were dazzling in the lights of the evening bazaars, and the profusion of merchandise, food and humans walking, running, cycling or driving recklessly through the cramped streets would normally have made me want to shut my eyes and ears. But I walked in a bubble of almost eerie silence as if I were listening very carefully for something.

Gabriel strolled beside me; I noticed how long his arms were in relation to his legs and body. How they swung slightly as they hung at his side; how his hands curved at the end of those overlong arms; how his head moved from side to side as if he were listening for something too, as if we had both heard something back in the square or the studio and it needed careful processing. Once or twice, I found myself staring at his hands, wanting to brush myself surreptitiously against them, or at least to move my hands closer to the space his hands occupied.

Almost involuntarily, I began to edge towards him in the crush of pedestrians.

Hands. For me, they carried the same kind of signal that a peacock carried in his feathers; I was, I often thought, a peahen for hands. I knew I was attracted to someone when I found myself stealing glimpses at their hands. There were no particular hands that I thought more beautiful than others. But as others might read the soul in a person's eyes – or in a person's photographs – I saw something inward in the hands: the way they occupied their space; the ease they might have as the fingers worked in relation to the palms. I could see more than what short thick fingers might mean, or long carefully manicured ones. What they did for work with those hands also mattered little, although I had once seen a butcher's hands so thick and stained that I couldn't help but envisage the dead flesh with which he worked for hours each day. Yet I had also observed hands that had toiled in the soil during years of manual labour that were as agile and elegant as a dancer's hands might be.

I'd had a similar perception when watching the 1998 World Cup, in which the French-Algerian player Zinedine Zidane was the star player. Watching Zidane move the football around the field with his feet was like watching something deeply internal become manifest in action. It felt possible to perceive his life story in the movement of his legs and feet – the deep pride, the intense focus, the ability to slow everything down, to direct so elegantly the flow of movement around him. I thought of him then in Kathmandu because there were traces of Zidane about Gabriel: the same bald, oddly shaped head; the same internal drive; the same ability to move things around according to his rhythm. He had, after all, managed to move someone as stubborn and self-directed as I was for hours, over my protests and malingering, until his instincts had steered us to the temple, and then the studio. These same instincts now seemed to create that bubble of silence for our route back to the hotel, as he swung his hands unobtrusively at his sides in a way that made me want to hold them.

My own hands were, as my mother might say, nothing to write home about. The nails on each finger and thumb were bitten. I was ashamed of them and would often curl my hands up if I was talking to someone, or gesture so quickly that people couldn't focus on my nails in the flurry of movement. It was impossible, though, to hide their scars from anyone for long. I used my hands in private and public: to play guitar, to type words, to strum my violin, to communicate to people.

At the same time, they were noteworthy for other reasons. They were small hands, almost tiny. And despite the hours and hours of creative and musical work my hands had done, they were not noticeably muscled, callused or distorted in any way. Their small size didn't seem to inhibit their span either. I could easily stretch wider than an octave on the piano, and though fingered octaves on the violin had always proved difficult for me, it was more to do with coordination than hand span.

We stopped at a small footpath café close to Durbar Square for dal bhat, a local specialty. As we waited, Gabriel turned to me, his face creased into a smile.

So you see, you never know, do you? he said in his stumbling, cryptic way, as if he had just picked up a train of thought he had left idling hours ago, not so much pleased with himself as relieved perhaps that all the twists and turns he had led me through had ended up somewhere tangible. *Didn't I tell you?*

Tell me what? I replied, not able to help smiling too.

He replied almost shyly. *That I would show you somewhere beautiful.*

Yes, you did. You certainly did tell me, I taunted him. *Quite a few times actually.*

Well then. What do you think?

You told me. And you showed me, I answered, suddenly re-energised by the thought of sharing a meal with Gabriel. *Now let's eat!*

After a severe bout of dysentery, the thought of food still

made me want to throw up most days, but now my mouth was literally watering in anticipation as I ordered a Nepali thali: a plate of dal, a selection of three vegetable curries, rice and pappadums.

Gabriel ate with his hands, Nepali and Indian style. I asked for a fork and parcelled the food carefully into my mouth, remembering the effects of the last full meal I had dared eat. To my surprise, though, the taste of the curries unfurled pleasurably.

Oh my God, I spluttered, shaking my head in wonderment.

See …? So beauty, he said, enjoying my enjoyment of my food. *You eat like a bird. But perhaps this is okay? Perhaps you sing like one too?*

I laughed, unable to make any coherent sound because of the food I kept stuffing into my mouth. As I ate my meal, I observed how Gabriel ate his. I noticed how his hands, covered in yellow curries, still managed to look clean and spatially elegant. Spatially elegant: I had never heard or used the phrase before. At least I didn't believe I had. It was an invention inspired by my companion and his hands, as we shared a meal in the Nepali night.

So, Gabriel said when we had finished our thalis. *How long are you in Kathmandu?*

Ten days, I told him. *I've been here three days, so seven to go.*

Seven. It was a good number. The number of colours in a rainbow. The number of basic notes in western and

Indian scales. The number of scholars and yogis. And, some say, the number of spiritual perfection.

Seven days was all I imagined I would have to get to know Gabriel. And perhaps all I would need.

And then, as I had many times with other travellers, I would say goodbye at an airport or a bus or train station. After our emotional goodbyes we would exchange emails, daily at first, then more sporadically, until their frequency petered out to nothing. There was nothing unexpected in such ebbs and flows of love and affection. It was the decorum of travel to understand the impermanence of connection – to not cling or expect anything long-term from these encounters, no matter how poignant or beautiful, but to celebrate and honour them, without hope or regret, as they arrived and departed. These were also the gifts of travel, the freedom not to possess or be possessed. To move, and love, as freely as a bird might sing its sad and joyful song.

My Summer of Peripheries

In the summer of 2005, I was staying in my friend Estelle's apartment in Ménilmontant, in the twentieth arrondissement of Paris, north-east of Saint-Paul. The apartment was on the top floor of an old building about halfway along the narrow cobblestone street. As such, its windows were perfect for gazing onto the street or across the skyline of the city. One evening I was sitting in the window alcove, looking down towards the main road, when I heard some accordion music coming from the block of apartments opposite me.

I listened for a bit and thought I recognised the music, which in many ways sounded to me a lot like Paris. Or the idea of Paris that so many foreigners have, of somewhere poetic, romantic, wistful, charming. You know that place: Paris, where gypsies play in the Métro, and the *bateaux* glide under bridges that double as outdoor stages for an astonishing array of musicians from all parts of the world, sometimes playing end to end on a Sunday when all the tourists crowd around Notre Dame as if they were walking in a dream.

After a few more fanciful minutes, I realised I wasn't listening to original or improvised music but something I had heard before. I listened a bit more until I recognised it as the accordion music from *Amélie*, the quirky film set in Paris starring Audrey Tautou, which had been a hit in Australia a few years before. I remember what a delight the film had been and how everyone wanted an Amélie haircut after the film came out. They wanted to dress like her too. I also recalled reading that tickets to Paris had experienced an upsurge after the success of the film. It seemed for a while then that everyone wanted that cinematic experience of Paris – nostalgic, retro, beautifully lit, with a denouement where love, despite all odds, wins out.

It was kind of a weird postmodern moment, being perched on the window ledge of a Parisian apartment listening to the accordion music from a film that constituted so many people's visions of Paris. Apart from the accordion music, the elements of the movie form a checklist of ingredients for 'a soufflé of Parisian delights', as one critic described the film:

characters whose lives revolve around a café (check)
in Montmartre (check),

an eccentric young woman (check)

with love (check!)

in all its permutations (check)

on her highly imaginative mind (check)

who acts as a love catalyst for an array of odd and/or
     sexy and/or curmudgeonly French people (check),

but who is challenged to open up her own heart to an
     equally adorably awkward boy she worships from
     afar …

even though he works in a porn shop somewhere in
     Paris.

Check!

Check!!

Check!!!

Ah Paree, enchanté! Ooh là là!

You can almost hear the bad French clichés emanating
from foreign tongues – mine included – when you watch
it. It was the kind of film foreigners loved, but which many
Parisians I knew were ambivalent about. They worried that
it contained the same kind of caricatures that I cringe about
in comparable Australian films, like *Crocodile Dundee*:

the cork hats,

big knives,

alligator skins and

taciturn men of the land.

That evening the music from *Le Fabuleux Destin d'Amélie
Poulain*, the film's original French title, was coming from an

upper-storey apartment across the narrow street. I followed the sound carefully and decided that it originated in the third apartment from the left on the fourth floor. The occupants obviously loved the music – and probably the movie too – because they played the CD often.

The night I first heard it, they were playing it when I went down the road to buy a felafel roll from the Turkish restaurant on the corner, and they were still playing it when I climbed back up the narrow staircase into the tiny but perfectly arranged apartment I'd been lucky enough to sublet for the summer, while Estelle was working on her PhD in Australia. They had it on repeat as I unwrapped my roll and savoured it slowly by the most subtle moonlight I had ever witnessed.

Who ever heard of a moon in daylight, I whispered, with my mouth impolitely full, to the northern-hemisphere moon. *Begone, moon, until it's properly dark.*

It was 9.30 pm and still light. But the moon was out in a kind of optical illusion conjured up by the same kind of creative mind behind *Le Fabuleux Destin d'Amélie Poulain*, the type of mind that loved contradictions and quirkiness and putting moons in inappropriate places.

Despite my intermittent telling-off of the moon, it was still a beautiful way to have dinner, serenaded by accordions as I ate my roll at the window ledge, looking across the rooftops of a city whose rooftops had so often been memorialised by poets, artists, photographers, philosophers and filmmakers.

Enough has been said about you, I whispered to the chimneys of Paris, as I picked some shredded lettuce out of my teeth. *There's nothing more to say. I will just enjoy you in this moment without making you a memory.*

I had eaten like this – and conversed with the white moon and chimneys and rooftops – almost every night since I'd arrived in Paris from a sweltering New Delhi three weeks before. I'd had memorable adventures in India and left Delhi reluctantly, even though there'd recently been bomb explosions in a crowded bazaar a few doors down from the hotel where I was staying. In contrast, Paris had felt safe, though unseasonably cold and surprisingly empty. Despite its relative security I missed the teeming chaos of the subcontinent and felt strangely bereft as I walked the quiet streets during my first weeks in the city.

A couple of nights after I first heard the music from *Amélie*, I heard it again. I was perched like a bird at the window and realised that the accordion apartment was hosting a gathering that night – a small group of friends, I assumed, judging by the clinking glasses and laughter wafting through the air between their apartment and mine. I imagined the scene as a French filmmaker might have depicted it: a party of casually elegant Parisians, dressed in shades of grey, blue, beige and black (which I'd already noticed were the classic colours of the city), while a woman sitting alone, looking at the Paris skyline, listens to the party from across the street. What is she thinking? What are her dreams? Will she find a way to cross the divide between herself and the Parisians at the party? Will she stop scolding the moon and find true love? Or at least a palatable philosophy – or a small, bearded philosopher perhaps – with which to make meaning of her solitude?

People often assumed I was lonely when I was alone. But travelling to new places made me feel as if I was ensconced in a fresh embrace and I felt restful sitting there. Paris could feel like a tranquil oasis, an oasis of music, what's more. Since I'd been in the city I'd noticed it everywhere, an urban soundtrack that had become the compensation for what I missed from India, whose melee of sounds had been absorbed into my skin so deeply I was in withdrawal for days after my jet lag had subsided.

The music of Paris came from India too, but also from other places – Africa, South America, Eastern Europe, Vietnam, Japan and China. It was alternately rhythmic and melodic, and old-fashioned in its own way. But that was Paris too: a conservator of antiquities, an archivist of what might otherwise be discarded. It cared about culture, and while the world raced ahead with its cutting-edge technology, abandoning its legacies in the process, Paris elegantly brought up the rear as it gathered up the sounds, the art, the stories of everywhere, and carried them back home to display in its museums and galleries, to read in its *bibliothèques* and bookshops, and to perform in its clubs and bars, conservatories and concert halls.

The city seemed to nestle the music of the globe in its arms; it gave space to a prodigious array of sounds, even that of the bearded philosopher with his homemade bicycle-powered instrument who pontificated on Pont Marie every weekend. I liked to roam and wander in search of music, and in Paris the odyssey uncovered a feast to be savoured, often randomly, in the streets, along the boulevards, on the trains, across the bridges, and through the cafés and restaurants. And now, as I could hear, in the homes of ordinary Parisians.

The sound of the accordion was pure and resonant as it travelled across the air: the speakers playing the *Amélie* music were obviously of very high quality. Or so I thought. Halfway through one of its most wistful phrases the music stopped. Perhaps a glitch in the CD, or a fault in the machine, I thought. Cutting off a melody unresolved always has an abrupt effect on my body and nervous system. I felt jangly and on edge: I had been halfway through a bite of my roll when the music came to a halt, and I felt unable to move until the music did.

The sound of the party increased a little. I imagined someone trying to repair the flaw and restart the music. Then I heard something quite unexpected. So unexpected that I still couldn't continue eating and hovered with my mouth wrapped around my dinner. Across the way, as if in surprise too, a small flock of pigeons took flight from the rooftop opposite. And down below a group of children began a game of catch on the footpath.

Mon Dieu! I called out telepathically to the birds. *What are we doing here? Re-enacting our favourite French film montages?*

What had so surprised me was the sound of the accordion going over some notes. I heard it again, then again, as if it were trying to gear itself up to begin afresh. It stopped once more and went back over a phrase, this time a different phrase. Then another. I recognised that sound. I had played enough live music to know what it meant, that mumbling of notes, that tentative repetition, those sketchy stumbles. I knew that the music wasn't coming from a CD player at all, but a real person playing a real accordion.

I dropped my felafel roll on the floor as I leaned out the window to listen. For some reason I was incredibly moved at the thought that I had been listening to a live musician playing a perfect re-creation of a CD recording.

Who does that? Who spends the time doing that? I whispered to the moon, which had the good sense to leave my question unanswered.

I didn't know that much about Paris yet. I had only been there for a relatively short time. But I felt I was experiencing something very particular about the city that I couldn't quite put my finger on.

I wondered if the accordionist lived in the apartment. Or was a visitor. Whether he or she played anything else but the music from *Le Fabuleux Destin d'Amélie Poulain*. Some Edith Piaf perhaps. Or music from further afield, an Astor Piazzolla tango maybe. Or if the music from the film was a private, very particular obsession, one that sometimes happens when an instrumentalist falls in love with a piece of music so deeply that they feel they and it are made for each other and spend hours, days and sometimes years making it theirs.

I stayed at the window late into the night, vicariously enjoying the party of Parisians and the live accordionist in their midst. I also spent some time whispering to the pigeons who sat on the ledge devouring the crumbs from my dishevelled dinner, which I'd salvaged from the floor soon after the music from *Amélie* started up again in all its melancholy, uplifting glory.

The next day I had arranged to meet Sebastian, a fellow musician I'd met in India, outside Notre Dame for a spot of busking. After the elation of the night before, I'd had a luxurious sleep-in and arrived at our pre-arranged meeting spot over an hour late. Too late for Sebastian, who was nowhere to be seen. I felt bad that I'd missed him but I didn't mind not busking that day. People love the idea of busking in Paris, a city in which it has such significance. But I'd done my time busking in Sydney's Kings Cross and I wasn't in any hurry to take out my violin here. I wanted different experiences now.

I sat down to rest for a few minutes before heading up to Rue de Rivoli at Saint-Paul to get the bus back to

Ménilmontant. I was in no hurry. That was my present to myself that summer – to be in no hurry in Paris. To let my days and nights unfold simply and easily. To not try so hard. To just be an audience for the things that might happen around me every moment. It had become a kind of discipline, this way of meeting experience.

Sometimes a city is the kind of place where, despite being on your own, you are never alone. Where sitting under a statue or leaning over the stone balustrade of a bridge is an invitation. You have to discern very quickly, though, who might waylay you, who might waste your time and who might be, like you, a pilgrim of the imagination on a voyage through change. But if your antenna is working properly, the chance encounter with a stranger might bring you something you need at that particular moment in time, something that might not come in any other part of the world, but exactly where your sense of wonder and curiosity has led you, across oceans and skies, out of safety into the unknown.

That summer in Paris, I'd already met many people by not hurrying, by taking my time, by resting next to a river, a statue, a gallery, a fountain. Or a cathedral, as I did that day at Notre Dame.

Fabian had come to play at Notre Dame as well. Not to busk like Sebastian, I fantasised when I laid eyes on him – à la Amélie Poulain – but perhaps to work on a song he was composing on his flamenco guitar, to while away those creative moments in the warm sun, to shape a melody among the soundwaves of the city rather than alone in his head, back in a tiny studio on the Left Bank.

He had found his spot to do that on the bench adjacent to where I was sitting with my violin case beside me. I had heard him before seeing him; heard the shimmer of strings as he strummed a few arpeggiated chords, the click of long flamenco fingernails on the banged-up wood of his instrument, his low breathy growl of a voice. I didn't have a clue what he was singing about, but the way he sang made me curious.

From the side I could tell he was tall and lanky enough to stretch out his legs and lazily cross them one on top of the other as they rested on his guitar case, which he had laid on the ground. On top of his angular profile a mop of curly brown hair, slightly flecked with grey, cascaded around his shoulders so that he looked both serious and carefree. He was dressed all in black – no surprise there, I thought – but on his feet he wore a pair of scuffed pointy blue suede shoes, as if he were ready to dance at any moment. All in all he looked like a grown-up pixie. A male Amélie, I thought delightedly, with an equally fabulous destiny that might, just then, for a few wondrous moments, intersect with mine.

I liked men who looked like spirit creatures with an intellectual bent and an adventurous approach to life. I liked the bravery that those qualities implied, the courage it took to always meet the new and unexpected. It never bothered me much what someone's physical appearance was like – I didn't really have a type; spirited men come in all shapes and sizes – or what nationality or age they were, or what they did for a living. What impressed me most was how they moved through the world. And from what I could see of his physicality and his body as he played music, I could tell that Fabian moved freely and, despite his angular roughness, with elegance too.

I didn't approach him though. Nor did I wait for him to approach me. I was quite happy just to notice his qualities and move on without ever speaking to him. I sat there quietly taking in my impressions of that iconic place, letting him breathe in his own space as I was breathing in mine, waiting for circumstances to move us closer together or further apart, without exerting too much will or effort. That was how I gauged if I was 'meant' to meet someone. In a world of travel and its endless possibilities, these little rules of engagement kept me centred and free from too many random entanglements.

You going inside, he suddenly called over.

Mmm? I asked, surprised out of my reflection by his deep French-accented voice.

Ooh là là, I thought to myself. *Now there is a voice. I could write a song about a voice like that. I could write a song with a voice like that.*

No, I don't think so, I called back.

Don't want to join the sheep then? he teased, laughing.

I like the outside. I laughed too.

Sorry? He swung his guitar up over his lap and leaned towards me so he could hear what I was saying over the hum of the crowds.

I like the outside … of things. Of buildings. Of monuments.

It was true. Since I'd arrived in Paris I'd hardly set foot inside a monument, but I'd spent a lot of time sitting outside them. Watching. Listening. Observing. Delighting. Enjoying the formations of people moving in and out of iconic places. Noticing how their faces changed from before they went inside, with all their dreams and fantasies, to when they emerged again into the light, blinking in wonder. During the last three weeks I'd sat outside Notre Dame, Saint-Paul-Saint-Louis, the Louvre and the Hôtel de Ville. I'd also walked around the Palais-Royal and the Musée d'Orsay, but I'd never gone inside. It was my summer of peripheries, I'd decided. My peripheral summer.

Mon Dieu, I said silently to the stone cathedral. *I am becoming an eccentric with my whims about entering things.*

I didn't quite know how to explain any of this to Fabian, but he was a musician like me, so I gave it a try. *I like to see and hear what's going on outside the centre of things. Outside the institution.*

Ah. You are a philosopher, he said humorously.

Depends what kind, I teased back.

I don't know, he replied, amused. *If you like the outside then maybe you are working on a philosophy of peripheralities. At the Sorbonne perhaps.*

I don't know how to describe it.

You're in Paris. We're good at categorising things.

Doesn't everybody like to think they're un-categorisable?

Mmm. Let me try. I am sure I can label you in a few moments.

Bet you can't, I challenged him.

He looked me over – in a friendly way, I was pleased to notice. *You are a violinist?*

Used to be.

And now you just like to carry around a case. Like a prop.

No, there's still a violin inside.

So you used to play.

I used to play … inside places like this. I waved at Notre Dame. *In churches and concert halls and opera houses. But then I walked outside and started playing on the streets and kind of never went back in.*

Ah. You are a refugee. He was teasing me again. I didn't mind.

Not really, though I suppose once you do go outside, I mused, *there's really no way back in.*

What did you leave? And why? No. Don't answer. It's not important. Well, you have come to the right place. The right city to wait for your documentation. Sooner or later most refugees come to Paris. They've been coming for centuries.

I laughed. *I don't need documentation. It's just my personal whim, I suppose. What my parents used to call my wilfulness. It's creative, not political.*

Of course it is. Music. Thoughts. Work. Love. Philosophy. You are in Paris now, ma chérie. Everything is political.

And with that pronouncement he strummed a few chords on his guitar and made me laugh again as a musical elf might, with a hint of mischief to come.

Ooh là là! I hummed along with his spontaneous song. *Here's trouble!* Just like my grandma would have said as she warned me off such a roguish boy. *With a capital T!*

Fabian didn't have a studio on the Left Bank. He was staying with friends at the Cité Internationale des Arts just across the Seine, which was on the way back to Saint-Paul and my bus home to Ménilmontant. So there was time to chat a little further before we parted. I found out that Fabian was only passing through Paris on his way to Marseilles and Barcelona, two places I'd never been to. He was on a musical odyssey, as I was, though mine was much more personal than his. He was following the gypsy trail inspired by the film *Latcho Drom*, which traced the journey of the Romani people through the musicians and dancers of India, Egypt, Turkey, Romania, Hungary, Slovakia, France and Spain.

He was intrigued to find out I'd come from New Delhi, where I was scheduled to return in September on my way back to Kathmandu, two cities he was yet to visit, and where the gypsy trail of *Latcho Drom* led in the other direction.

As for his fluency in English, which was remarkable among all the French people I'd met so far (except for Estelle, who was brilliantly bilingual), Fabian proudly explained he'd spent four years in high school in England and was therefore fluent in every English vulgarity known to humankind. As we walked I also discovered to my great amusement that Fabian seemed to have some kind of photographic memory, or at least a catalogue in his brain, about places in Paris and their history. When I told him I was staying in Ménilmontant, he reeled off an array of information about the area: that it was affectionately called Ménilmuche by locals; that it was the birthplace of Maurice Chevalier and the next suburb along from Belleville, where Edith Piaf used to sing on the footpaths; that the main character of *Les Enfants du Paradis*, the beautiful tragic Garance, comes from Ménilmontant; and that *The Red Balloon*, which was still shown to new generations of children, was filmed there in 1956, as was, years later, a chase scene from *The Bourne Identity*.

What are you, a Wiki nerd? I joked.

Of course not. In France we chop off the heads of such superficial researchers. But though I sometimes hate this city I love it too. And like an attentive lover I want to know all about my lady. So now we at least know you are in the right place for music and for dreaming, he assured me as we stopped for crepes near Pont Saint-Louis. *And what exactly are you doing here?*

Nothing really, I said, unable to define it, and concentrating for the moment on devouring my crepe, which was soft and sweet and dripping in honey. *Maybe I'll write some songs; that's what I usually do when I'm staying somewhere new.*

Ah, you're a singer then. Une chanteuse.

Not particularly. I mean I don't sing anything but my own songs. I only started singing so I could sing my own songs.

Ah! A singer of your own songs – a singer-songwriter. Une chanteuse-compositrice.

That sounds altogether too grand for me … une compositrice. Ooh là là. La-di-da! Anyway, at the moment I'm not doing anything really. I am just sitting at the window looking out and listening.

I told him about the night before.

Oh! Amélie Poulain. The number of girls that came to Paris with those haircuts, mooning around Montmartre waiting to be lovestruck. Or men looking for French girls who look like her. Sacré bleu! Makes me sick. Paris is not just sweet and nostalgic like eating this crepe in the shadow of Notre Dame. It is grit and work and difficulty. Century after century of it. So we can have this pretty shiny city today. We've fought hard for our sweetness. We've cut off the heads of kings for these fantasies.

I waited while he got his rant out of his system. Eventually he calmed down and we began heading up to Pont Marie.

Anyway, standing at your window is a very good place to be. Listening is good too.

He looked me over again as if he was trying to read me. I smiled and spoke through a mouthful of crepe. *But you still can't categorise me, right?*

He smiled in response. Ruefully. *Give me time.*

You're running out. We're nearly there.

So, he began shyly. *What you're saying is you don't want to see me again. Is that correct?*

I giggled. Yes, I actually giggled. He was such a sweet rogue and he brought out the rogue in me. *I'm just hoping you're not going to ask me if I've got a Parisian lover yet.*

Ooh là là … Why do you think I'm going to ask you that? No. Don't answer. Let me use my powers of deduction to guess. You are a woman on your own in Paris and so naturally you are in the market for a boyfriend. Some would consider it their duty as Frenchmen to make sure lonely women are … assisted. It's just chivalry.

I'm not lonely. I am alone, but I often find I am not lonely. I am always ready to meet the world. Besides, as my mum used to say, I have other things on my mind.

He looked at me hard then, as if he were peering right through me. *Yes. I can tell … that if you didn't want to be, you would not be alone.* He beamed, elfish again. *And I see your mother was right. You have many things on your mind. Many beautiful things. Anyway, for your information, I wasn't going to ask you if you'd found your Parisian lover yet.*

Good.

Really?

Yes, really.

Most women want to be seduced. Most men want to seduce. That little scenario is like a happily co-dependent couple dancing through time.

There's more of a chance to get to know you without seduction.

He grinned. *Interesting angle … for many, seduction would be a way of getting to know someone.*

We both laughed. Our conversation was like the sharp easy exchange of rhythm, meaning and melody that musicians sometimes make, enabled by listening and flow and a kind of inherent sensitivity to the other. Which is another way of saying that we were beginning to make some kind of beautiful, and quite unexpected, music together, swinging our instrument cases as if they were as light as feathers while we walked over Pont Marie across the sparkling Seine, up towards Rue de Rivoli.

We were still laughing as we arrived at the bus stop just near Saint-Paul.

This is me, then.

He stood back, his eyes quizzical. *This most certainly is you. I don't doubt it. But who or what that is, I can't quite put my finger on … yet.* He looked at me intently again.

My bus, I meant. I felt shy at his gaze but not threatened in any way.

We both ummed and ahhed for a few seconds in a flurry of mutual, delighted embarrassment brought on by a shyness I couldn't understand. A moment or two passed before he broke the awkwardness.

Anyway, what I was going to ask is if you have found a Parisian guitarist yet.

I laughed. In relief. And then laughed some more in delight and recognition. Perhaps he was a kindred soul, this mischievous-spirited man.

No ... I haven't. I usually play alone. But you've surprised me. I didn't expect that. Most people look at my violin and ask if I'll play with them. Not if they can play with me ... if you get the difference.

Vive la différence, mon amie. I'm curious to see what you do.

Still want to categorise me then?

I would be honoured.

My bus arrived. I didn't say anything as I got on and found a seat next to an open window. Fabian was smiling as he looked eagerly in my direction, waiting for me – willing me, perhaps – to lean out of the window and call out something significant as a way of saying *au revoir*. Instead I threw out some of the most clichéd words in the world, ones I'd heard a million times in films and television shows. Or read in countless books about love and adventure and chance encounters. Words which, up to that point in my life, I'd never had a chance to say to anyone.

Same time, same place. In two days' time!

The bus was pulling out when the meaning of my words slowly dawned on Fabian's face. He waved and bowed and mouthed some words in a singular, seamless flourish, which was something like a particularly unexpected and unique phrase of music.

I'll be there. I will be there. Wouldn't miss it for the world! He laughed as he mouthed the words, trotting beside the moving vehicle, his guitar case grasped in one hand, the other waving at me, as the bus to Ménilmontant turned and joined the Parisian peak-hour traffic, heading up towards what suddenly and equally unexpectedly felt like home.

Revolution at the Peace Hotel

One Sunday afternoon in November 2011, about two weeks before I was due to leave Shanghai, I went to high tea at the Peace Hotel with my friends Sue and Gerard. They were in town for a few days and having high tea was the kind of thing they did. Not me. Not usually anyway. I was living on a budget: most nights in Shanghai I would either cook in the tiny kitchen in my room or eat around the corner from my hotel in Zhongshan Park at the Uyghur Restaurant. This was a cultural as well as a culinary experience. The Uyghurs, Muslims from the north-west of China, were sometimes considered troublesome by the authorities. Despite this, their food was very popular in Shanghai – among expats, Shanghainese and travellers. It was cheap, oily and very very tasty. It was also markedly different from the usual Cantonese-style cuisine available in many restaurants in the area. I favoured the spinach and garlic dishes, the fried egg with tomato, the chilli cucumber and yoghurt, the traditional flat bread baked in a clay oven on the footpath and the buttery boiled rice.

It was the type of food I would never eat back home, where I lived on a mostly vegan diet. But I had abandoned my pristine habits for the pleasure of walking out of the hotel lobby, especially as the nights became colder, heading down Huichuan Road, rounding the corner and arriving at the small, grimy restaurant with its slightly acrid smells and warm chaos. I loved the large family who ran the place – the plump, partially veiled matriarch, and her young son, with whom I would play a few squealing games of hide-and-seek as I waited for my food to be prepared in what would never be deemed an hygienic kitchen back in Australia. I loved the Afghani-influenced music playing on their radio speakers all night; the mischievous, instinctive swaying of hips in time with the drumbeat that sometimes overtook us all; and the intricate mime I developed with the waiters, young men from the Uyghur provinces who spoke neither English nor much Mandarin, but a kind of hybrid Urdu.

High tea at the Peace Hotel was something else altogether. It was scrupulously clean for a start, and there was definitely no hide-and-seek happening on its shiny marble floors. The atmosphere was resonant of colonial days. Still, it wasn't only westerners who filled the plush high-tea area on the Sunday afternoon I met Sue and Gerard there. Along with the well-heeled tourists and expats were many Chinese, obviously wealthy, some of whom were clothed in the ostentatious designer gear – the kind with brand names prominently displayed – that seemed all the rage in Shanghai then.

The high tea was an elegant spectacle: the waiters and waitresses costumed like servants, the opulent decor superbly detailed, and the maître d'hôtel hovering like a director around his beautifully postured actors. After being in the country for two months, it was clear to me that the Chinese were brilliant at form and aesthetics. You only had to sit through one of the lake performances overseen by the award-winning director Zhang Yimou – I'd seen two, each of them perfect – or recall the awe-inspiring pyrotechnics of the Beijing Olympic opening ceremony to understand the country's gift for precision and order. At the Sunday afternoon high tea, the staff manufactured the kind of serenity that the old colonial powers liked to conjure up in these establishments. And despite the convulsive previous century, the Chinese showed at the Peace Hotel one of the things they do best: creating a sense that everything was in its proper place, that there was nothing to worry or protest about. The tea would arrive hot, the cakes fresh; the chatter would remain barely audible; the hierarchies in place were working for everyone; and all would be well in the world.

During the afternoon, I sipped English breakfast tea and nibbled on petits fours, occasionally dipping into the conversation between my friends, who were experienced travellers. They were discussing the recent stand-off between Qantas management and its employees, an industrial brouhaha that had made the news even in China. Sue and Gerard were on the side of management, describing the rolling strikes that had preceded the shutdown as 'death by a thousand cuts'. I'd been following the saga on CCTV, one of the two English-language news channels available at my hotel, but that afternoon I was more interested in the young woman playing the guqin in a corner of the room. The guqin is a traditional Chinese stringed instrument that is plucked and strummed as it lies lengthways across the instrumentalist's lap. Even though it was made of wood and metal, this guqin was balanced gracefully across its player's lap as if it were made of silken cloth. The musician had a pretty, soulful face that matched the kind of music she was playing. I was entranced – with the sound of the instrument, with the musician, and with how this elegant detail fitted into the high-tea experience.

The musician looked up and noticed me noticing her. We smiled shyly at each other, and nodded. I used to play background music on afternoons such as these, in my days as a freelance classical musician, so I knew the hierarchy of such employment. You must look and sound beautiful and tasteful. Preferably you are in a corner, as the guqin player was, your sound is as unobtrusive as possible, and you play repertoire that is familiar. Listening to her so intently, then, was almost a subversive act. I didn't know the music she was playing. But I recognised its genre, a sweeping folk melody that was both poignant and rousing, a combination at which the Chinese also seemed to excel.

During her next break I went over and asked her about the music. Like many Chinese she preceded our conversation with an apology for her bad English, but she spoke it well. She introduced herself by her English name, Miriam.

After a few polite exchanges I asked if she played music full time.

No, she told me, *I am actually a doctor.*

Of music?

She shook her head. *Of traditional Chinese medicine.*

TCM, I echoed her reply as its acronym. Ever since I'd arrived in China I'd been trying to find a good TCM doctor. Most Chinese I'd asked, though, didn't know of any. They all went to western doctors. It had become a kind of running joke, made more ironic when I divulged that back home I usually only saw a Chinese doctor, and that for most common health problems I took herbs or had acupuncture.

You're studying? I asked. She looked so young.

No, I am a fully qualified doctor, she smiled sweetly. *But many people ask me that. It is the reason why I can't practise medicine.*

What do you mean?

I had a job in two hospitals and in each place the patient would ask for another doctor – an older doctor, a man doctor. They didn't think someone who looked like me could practise medicine.

I wanted to ask her more about this. But I noticed the maître d'hôtel hovering and didn't want to pry further.

I changed the subject back to music. I told her about my journey around the world singing and researching love songs. She told me the next piece she was going to play was based on a famous story about two star-crossed lovers from warring families who die tragically and turn into butterflies. Many traditional Chinese folk songs were about love: lost, unrequited, tragic, haunting, eternal love.

The two lovers are like the Chinese version of Juliet and Romeo, she explained. *They both die and become butterflies and fly away and live together for a long time.*

She sighed.

But I don't really know if such a love exists, she continued, surprisingly philosophical. *Though I keep looking.*

I thought I saw or heard her tear up. But she bowed her head, so I couldn't tell if she really was crying. Or if she just had a voice or face that easily carried a tremor. I wondered if she'd had a recent break-up. I gently asked if I could make a recording of the piece on the Zoom recorder that I carried around with me most days. If she allowed me to record the music, I promised to make her a copy. She agreed.

As I expected, the song was sweet, sad and soulful, with plucked tremolo, tragic motifs and cascades of sound that washed through the hotel.

After she finished 'The Butterfly Lovers', she segued into another piece, and I noticed Sue and Gerard getting up to leave. I nodded goodbye to Miriam – whose fingers, I noticed, moved like butterflies across the strings – and indicated I would see her again soon. She smiled serenely as I turned back to my friends and walked out with them.

We were all talking about how much we loved Shanghai when, around the corner from the lobby, I noticed some stairs leading upwards. On the wall at the foot of the stairs there was a sign that read *Peace Hotel Gallery ... Hours Available.*

It was nearly closing time. But I was so intrigued by the prospect of a Peace Gallery that I excused myself and walked up the stairs to find out what such a place would reveal about the hotel's history.

The gallery was a small room lined with neatly framed photos above a series of glass display cabinets. As I began walking across the room, a jovial-looking man wearing a uniform introduced himself as the director of the gallery. His name was Mr Martin Ma, and he had worked at the hotel for nearly fifty years. When I asked if I could record our conversation about the hotel's history, he was initially suspicious of me – as many Chinese officials usually are of a westerner holding a recording device. But after reassuring him I was a writer, not a journalist, a difference that he interpreted as significant, he relaxed.

For the next half-hour I learned about the hotel, which had been built by Victor Sassoon, a rich Jewish businessman. When it first opened in 1929, it was called the Cathay Hotel, and it became an important part of the 'gateway to China' role that Shanghai played for over a century.

During his commentary Martin referred convivially to many famous names as if he personally knew them. Charlie Chaplin came with his *Great Dictator* co-star Paulette Goddard, when they couldn't stay at other hotels – they weren't married at the time. Noël Coward wrote his gloriously plaintive song 'Someday I'll Find You' during one of his stays and, according to folklore, wrote his play *Private Lives* in four days during another visit when he was confined to his bed with the flu. Mary Pickford and Douglas Fairbanks were also visitors – in the fading days of their superstardom – as was George Bernard Shaw. Steven Spielberg did location shoots at the hotel when he was making *Empire of the Sun*, adapted from JG Ballard's book about his experiences in Shanghai during the war.

The roll call of famous visitors was rich and historically significant, and Martin spoke delightfully – and delight-edly – about the foreign dignitaries, prime ministers, presidents and leaders who had visited the Peace Hotel: Gough Whitlam, Paul Keating, Bill and Hillary Clinton,

Richard Nixon and Henry Kissinger, to name but a few. He became more sombre, but only slightly, when he told of how the Japanese occupied the hotel during the war and set up headquarters in Victor Sassoon's private suite, causing the magnate to flee. He brightened, though, when he divulged that, despite a bomb exploding on the street right outside, the hotel itself remained unscathed during the war.

The Communist Revolution in 1949 was bad for business at the hotel, as many wealthy Chinese exiled themselves to Hong Kong, Europe, America and Australia. As foreign investment in China dried up, the hotel had to be closed in 1952, before re-opening four years later as the Peace Hotel, named after an international peace conference in Beijing. Hotel guests steadily returned as overseas visitors came back to Shanghai, but they fled again during the Cultural Revolution, as foreigners were regarded as the imperialist dogs of Mao's propaganda apparatus.

After falling into disrepair during the last part of the twentieth century, the hotel was painstakingly renovated by the Fairmont hotel consortium for three years, and it re-opened to great fanfare in 2010. According to Martin, these days were the very best days the hotel – and Shanghai itself – had ever seen. I was pleased to hear this after all the turmoil the hotel had been through; pleased for Martin, whose loyalty to his place of employment was charming and touching.

The consortium had pledged to restore the Peace Hotel – now the Fairmont Peace Hotel – to its former glory. It was certainly a fantastic place to stay, in the heart of Shanghai's famous Bund area, which overlooked the newly constructed district of Pudong. Pudong, which had been hardly more than a fishermen's swamp ten years before, now resembled a sparkling alien world, with buildings created by some of the world's top architects who had vied for the challenge of designing a high-tech, feng shui–inspired business district. This was modern Shanghai, the place whose development made the Chinese proud but commentators all over the world anxious. In newspapers and blogs, they would tut-tut that every expansion heralded an eventual contraction, that every rapid rise preluded a meteoric collapse.

As Martin guided me back to the stairs, I held out my hand to say goodbye. He grasped it warmly, and pointed to some photos on the far wall. He then led me across the room to a black-and-white photograph of a band of elderly Chinese jazz players.

Martin asked if I preferred younger music and musicians. I told him I thought older jazz players were better because they had played more, seen more, heard more.

There was a topic that had haunted me since I'd arrived in China, one that few Chinese people would discuss with me. *I heard that in Shanghai in the Cultural Revolution*, I began mischievously, *you could still hear jazz in some small bars hidden away in the back streets of the city.*

Shanghai had always considered itself different, more cosmopolitan than the rest of China – the Shanghainese I knew prided themselves on it. They were the New Yorkers of China, living on an island of sophistication in a country of proletariat and peasants. So that story hadn't surprised me.

Martin responded emphatically. *No*, he said. *That is not possible. There was no jazz. No European music or American music at that time. In the revolution they stopped the western music. We only had the Chinese music. Like* White-Haired Girl, *a very famous ballet. It tells a story about a girl who loved a boy. But a rich landlord asked her to marry him. The girl loved her boy, though, so she went into the mountains rather than marry. After many years her black hair turned to white because she was away so long waiting for her lover to find her. When the village was liberated by the communists her boyfriend met her in the mountains and took her back to the village.*

I wondered aloud if love had turned her white hair back to its original colour.

Martin laughed. *Of course her hair didn't change back. But thanks to the Communist Revolution the story had a happy ending, I think.* White-Haired Girl *is what we call a typical drama. We had eight typical dramas in the Cultural Revolution. Do you know about them?*

I told him that I knew very little about the Cultural Revolution, although I imagined people from the west would discuss it more often than those in China. During my first week in the country, though, I had sat next to a professor from Fudan University – Shanghai's premier university – and he told me he had been reassigned to manual labour during the Cultural Revolution because all the universities and schools had been shut down. If he had ever been outraged by his fate, he seemed sanguine about it now. *What's done is done. The past is gone*, he mused over dinner.

It had been a bad time for intellectuals, academics and artists. There'd been violence, suicide, horrible torture and savage humiliations. Old China against New China – that was the official line. In truth, the Red Guards, mostly young hotheads, were let loose in a brutal suppressive rampage across the country, and Mao apparently had done nothing to stop them. The old professors, young poets and budding intellectuals didn't stand a chance in this cultural onslaught on China's most revered traditions. Confucianism was derided, the old Buddhist philosophies were discredited, and so was the old literature. Western influences were abhorred as decadent. The country still couldn't officially discuss it. Like much of its recent history, the Cultural Revolution felt like a deep psychic wound that the authorities seemed fearful to acknowledge.

I guessed that Martin would have been just a boy during that time. And that, as a humble worker at the Peace Hotel, he'd have been spared the brutality of the revolution. It seemed that way as he continued his story.

They closed the universities because no one wanted to learn English – they were too busy doing revolution. So there were no more lessons.

He was matter-of-fact, giving no indication that his dialogue was about to veer off the official line towards something more personal to him.

At the time an American who taught at the Shanghai Foreign Language Institute came here. During the revolution it wasn't safe for her there. So the institute brought her here and she stayed in the hotel. She was an African-American.

He spoke with a kind of triumphant pride. I didn't know if his pride was connected to the colour of the American professor's skin or to the unfolding context of the story.

How long did she stay at the hotel? I asked.

She came here in 1967 and she stayed for over a year. She found the room service waiters couldn't speak good English and volunteered to teach them. She taught two classes, a beginners' class and a medium class. I was an interpreter for beginners and a student in the medium class. I learned my English from her. I am speaking to you today, I have this job, because of her.

He beamed fondly at the memory of his former teacher.
You want to know her name?

I did, although I didn't expect to recognise it.

Her name was Garvin, Vicki. Vicki Garvin. Do you know her?

I shook my head.

I have had no contact with her since she left in 1968. I hope she is okay and her health is in very good condition. I think she'd be more than eighty years old now. It's a long time ago.

He seemed so eager to find out about Vicki Garvin that I offered to Google her name and see what that turned up.

My offer excited him. *I have waited a long time to know what happened to her. But maybe today everything changes. Maybe you will help me get some information.*

He continued reminiscing. *You know she wrote the texts herself. She used simple things we could understand, like the descriptions of the rooms here at the Peace Hotel, to teach us. Also the quotations of Chairman Mao. You want to know one I especially remember?* He giggled. *What is work? Work is struggle.*

Oh yes, he concluded. *Life is very interesting. Isn't it? I still have the book that she typed. I typed it out for everybody.*

He laughed and laughed, spluttering as he did, as if his body couldn't contain the memories of forty-seven years of work at the Peace Hotel, and all the violence and joy and extraordinary encounters which that history had contained.

We said goodbye warmly at the top of the stairs. I promised again to do what I could to find information about Vicki. I also promised to come back the following week with a CD copy of the recording I had taken of his tour.

I left the Peace Hotel as if in a dream. As if I had been touched by history in a way I couldn't yet understand.

The gift of stories, of listening to and receiving them, of being at the right place at the right time – all the magic of travel – warmed me down to my toes.

The walk back from the Bund to the subway station was the usual cacophony of tourists, hawkers, cars and motorcycles. But I felt like dancing down the Corso, humming Noël Coward's 'Someday I'll Find You' – a song my mother used to sing in our lounge room in Brisbane – as if I finally had found that elusive *you*. In this case, the *you* was not a lover, but a connection as warm and true as love, from a seemingly random encounter.

The neon seemed especially spectacular that evening. The deeply crimson reds, the iridescent blues, the glorious greens sparkled like they'd been conjured up in a CGI lab. The recent rain gave everything a kind of liquid haze. People might lament the modernisation of Shanghai – the loss of its heritage, the encroachment of business and western decadence. But to me the neon was magic. Like a fairyland. I was falling in love with this city more every day. I loved China too. I wanted it to do well, to thrive: this great, baffling, over-populated country with its collective sense of existence and its impersonal view of things. The vastness of its history made the serenity I'd found at the Peace Hotel that afternoon even more extraordinary.

I was determined to keep my promise to Martin, to repay him for his time that afternoon, and find out what I could about Vicki. I imagined I wouldn't find out much.

She had probably gone back to the States and disappeared into teaching life. The idealism that might have brought her to China in the '60s probably dissipated with the revelations of Mao's excesses. With any luck, though, she'd obtained a good tenured job that might show up on a quick Google search. A few lines from a university website might satisfy Martin, who probably only wanted to know if Vicki Garvin was still alive and if she had an email address where, after all these decades, he could contact her.

On my way back to my hotel, I stopped at Starbucks to order a takeaway latte. While I waited for my order, I chatted to Heidi, a tall, beautiful Chinese girl with a serious face, sad eyes and an occasional dazzling smile, who worked there most days and evenings. Like many of the Chinese I'd met, she worked long hours for little money. She was saving up to move out of her parents' home, a brave move for a single Shanghai girl. Heidi's name wasn't really Heidi. All the workers at Starbucks had chosen Anglicised names and all spoke a little English, to make the café more 'international'. She had named herself after Heidi Klum, the German supermodel, who, according to Chinese Heidi, was the epitome of grace and beauty: tall, blond, skinny, white.

I told her often she was ten times more beautiful than Heidi Klum or any of the supermodels she was obsessed with. But she said she didn't see how her *yellow skin, boring straight black hair and small eyes* could possibly be seen as beautiful.

As I waited for my takeaway, we talked about how she dreamed of going to Paris one day, and Berlin, and New York. But most of all the *coast of gold* in Australia. I told her I used to take Christmas holidays on the Gold Coast, that my family had a house there. She asked me to tell her about the place and whether the coast really was gold.

The sand was sometimes golden, I reminisced. *And sometimes the sun and the sky in the afternoon. There are beaches for miles all up and down the coast.*

She gasped with pleasure. *Of course*, she lamented, *it is almost impossible to afford to travel on my wages from Starbucks. And even if I had the money it's not so easy for us to travel out of China.*

I sympathised. It was a difficult time for Shanghainese like Heidi. Advertising and the curious financial system that the Chinese had branded 'communist capitalism' had brought western-type dreams. Yet visa and passport restrictions still made travelling difficult.

As she delivered my takeaway to me, I promised her I saw good luck in her future.

I was still sipping from the supposedly recycled container from Starbucks when I got back to my hotel room, opened my computer and Googled the name Vicki Garvin. I realised how difficult it must have been for Martin to find out any information about his former teacher. Most sites about her were blocked, but a few lines in one of the search results described her thus:

Victoria Garvin, African-American liberation
activist and dedicated internationalist, died on
June 11, 2007, after a long illness, at the age of 91.

I emailed the blocked links back to friends in Australia and
asked if they could paste the information from those sites
into their replies.

A day or so later I received two emails back. Each contained
similar information about a black American activist who went
by the name Vicki Ama Garvin. She had become a Maoist
sympathiser because of his avowed support of racial equality
at a time when African-Americans were still being lynched in
the South. Most interesting was this information, originally
from a Pan-African newsletter but now found on an anti-
imperialist news site – which, ironically enough, could not be
accessed by the anti-imperialist Chinese:

In 1964 Vicki was invited to China by the Chinese ambas-
sador. Both Malcolm X and Dr DuBois encouraged her
to go. She taught English for six years in Shanghai to
students and hotel workers. She became close friends with
many of her young students and kept in touch with them
over the years. In China, she also became close to then
political exiles Robert F Williams and Mabel Williams.
When Mao Tse-Tung issued his proclamation in support
of the Afro-American movement in 1968, Vicki made a
speech about the statement to a rally of millions. Also

in China she met and married Leibel Bergman in a Red Guard ceremony during the early days of the Cultural Revolution, and became a loving stepmother to his daughter and two sons.

Along with this text, there were two photographs of Vicki that had been used at her memorial in 2007. She was a striking woman: I was instantly drawn to her. The earlier photograph, in black and white, showed a slim, well-dressed woman with a regal posture and the natural beauty of a model. In the aura she exuded, she looked, as Barack Obama would many decades later, like someone who would make a difference. It was as if she had decided on work, engagement and action as the course of her life – as if she had been born knowing what needed to be done, and would always act and work for her people.

That knowledge came through in how she presented herself. In this photograph she was wearing a stylish white coat as she stood at an old-fashioned radio microphone, holding papers in her hand. Written on a banner draped across the platform was the partially hidden word *McCarthy*. Presumably this referred to the notorious anti-communist senator who instigated the witch hunts that led to the 'reds under the bed' hysteria in the US in the early '50s. Perhaps she was delivering a speech to rally African-American workers to fight for their civil rights – a cause she was dedicated to, as the accompanying text mentioned several times. I imagined that it must have been difficult to be Vicki Garvin in the Cold War years, and marvelled at her poise amid what must have been daily surveillance from the FBI and the CIA.

The second photograph was in colour and showed Vicki later in life as a warm, relaxed, almost jovial woman; her smile was bright, un-ironic; her eyes keenly intelligent. She was still stylish, wearing a silken green dress patterned with blue and crimson flowers; her short white hair was brushed back in a soft halo. She reminded me of my grandmother, who also had that bearing of someone who had agency – even though my grandmother had been terrified of communists, as many people were in Australia after the Second World War, and suspicious, in her Irish Catholic way, of people who held different political views.

I felt relieved looking at the older Vicki. For someone who had had to overcome many battles, with so much violence accompanying the revolutions that embodied her political ideals, she appeared to have her sense of peace and humour intact. Her clear, virtually unlined face had become even more dignified and beautiful – serene, friendly and without obvious bitterness.

Martin would be excited to learn all this: I immediately pasted this information into an email to him.

She was recognized by many organizations as an 'honored elder' for her contributions to the freedom struggle of her people and the world's peoples. In speeches made just before her serious health decline, Vicki urged the younger generations forward. She wrote: 'Of course there will be twists and turns, but victory in the race belongs to the long-distance runners, not sprinters. Everywhere the just slogan is reverberating – no justice, no peace!'

It seemed incredible that my seemingly random conversation with Martin had unlocked this information for him. I thought again of China and its collective sense of history, of the impression it worked so hard to give of order and harmony. What was going on underneath this populous country, I wondered, where folk songs about impossible love seemed embedded in the psyche? What about Martin's life had led him, with his memories and private wonderings, to ask a stranger about someone he once knew? Did he ask everyone who came into the gallery, or only those curious enough to take it further? And what about my life, lived out in the relative security of Australia, where the chances of encountering Vicki Garvin and her story were virtually nil, had led me to him?

Two days later I received an email back.

Date: Mon, 14 Nov 2011
Subject: RE: Vicki Garvin

Dear Linda,

You are so kind sending this text of Vicki Garvin to me. I will read it carefully and throughly. This is what I am looking for many many years. How it would be much better if I can find it earlier. But I am still so appreciated.

Martin Ma
Director of Peace Gallery

I replied at once and asked if he could provide some details about his own life, hoping to have a clearer picture about how it fitted into the tapestry of China's history.

I spent the next few days preparing the CDs to take back to the Peace Hotel. First, I made a clean recording of my interview with Martin. He had never heard himself speak and I imagined he might be taken aback. I spent a lot of time smoothing out his stumbles and hesitations, and editing out the bangs and clashes from in and around the Peace Gallery, so that his English sounded as clear and fluid as possible. His personality, so amiable in person, expressed itself even more impressively – and subtly – the more I listened.

I also spent some time on the recording I had made of 'The Butterfly Lovers'. The acoustics were already good and the playing was flawless, so all I did was add a little reverb to make the CD sound almost professional. An inquiry back to another friend in Australia had brought me this information:

The eight typical revolutionary operas were engineered by Mao's wife Jiang Qing, and were the only forms of artistic expression allowed in China during the Cultural

Revolution. Unlike the European western model, where opera was a form of bourgeois entertainment for the cultured and wealthy, the operas were made in accordance with Mao's provision that 'art must serve the interests of the workers, peasants, and soldiers and must conform to proletarian ideology'.

My last two weeks in Shanghai passed by quickly. So it was not until two days before I was about to leave the city that I returned to the Peace Hotel. In my bag I carried the two CDs I had promised my new friends: a recording of my conversation with Martin and a recording of 'The Butterfly Lovers' for Miriam. Martin was having one of his rare days off: I left the CD with his colleague who was that day in charge of the Peace Gallery. Miriam was in the middle of her recital when I arrived downstairs, so I had a chance once again to listen to the echo of the guqin as it reverberated through the lobby. Afterwards we sat together and, when I had given her the CD, she told me she had decided to go to New York to be with her American boyfriend. I wondered aloud whether it would be difficult for her to get a passport and visa to travel to the States. But she told me that in the new China, things like going and returning were not as difficult as they had once been. For her, America was not the land of plenty or the land of her dreams. It was a place like many other places, to visit and explore. She thanked me for the CD as we stood outside the Peace Hotel, about to head in opposite directions. She was going left up the Bund and I was headed right towards the train station where I would take the metro back to Zhongshan Park. The atmosphere was misty, and as I walked I noticed my eyes were too. I was glad I had left a memento of my visit with Martin and Miriam because I did not know if I would have the chance to return to Shanghai.

On the way back from the train station in Zhongshan Park to my hotel, I stopped in at Starbucks to say goodbye to my friends there. Heidi surprised me by gathering the staff around her and presenting me with a gift: a Starbucks mug with Shanghai emblazoned on the front. I hugged each of them; when I embraced Heidi, I promised to send her a similar mug back from the Gold Coast. *Ahh*, she sighed, *the coast of gold. I'll meet you there soon.*

*

Two days after Christmas, which I spent with my family at Brighton, a seaside suburb north of Brisbane, I received an email from Martin:

Date: Tue, 27 Dec 2011
Subject: thank you

Dear Linda,

I am really appreciated receiving your email in such a quickplay.

Now I answer your questions.

I was born in Shanghai at Hwang Pu District, a lane very closed the Jing An District and also near the Soochow Creek. There was a small temple near by, named Da Wang Miao (Temple of King). I can show you the place if you were interested at your next coming.

I got my first job of working in Peace Hotel, it wasn't found by myself, but assigned by the Lane Business Association after I graduate junior middle school at 18. Without interview, but health check-up before they accept me to enter.

Same as you miss Shanghai and especially the Peace Hotel, I really miss your return too and talk to you again.

Please feel free asking me if you have any query.

Sincerely Yours,

Martin Ma
Director of Peace Gallery

I hadn't been able to stop thinking about Martin and Vicki. I was eager to keep connecting all the threads of what seemed to be a bigger, more international story. After some ferreting on Google, I had managed to track down one of Vicki's surviving stepchildren, Lincoln Bergman. His father, Leibel Bergman, a prominent revolutionary and communist in the United States, had married Vicki in that

Red Guard ceremony. Lincoln was a broadcaster, teacher, writer and poet, and was also deeply devoted to left-wing causes. His first poem, written when he was eight, was a tribute to Ethel and Julius Rosenberg, and his website biography gave an extraordinary insight into life as a child of revolutionaries:

I live in Richmond, California, on a hill with a view of the Golden Gate and Bay bridges, and the San Francisco skyline when the fog lifts. I write to you from a yurt in our backyard.

I retired from Lawrence Hall of Science, a science and curriculum development center at UC Berkeley, in mid-2010, but still do some editorial work there ... I attended Deep Springs Jr. College – a unique liberal arts college and working cattle ranch, in Deep Springs Valley, two valleys up from Death Valley. I went on to junior year at Cornell University, living at Telluride House, in 1964/5.

The next year, thanks to my father's intense interest in and support of the Chinese revolution, I taught English to college students my age at the Institute for International Relations in the People's Republic of China (it was forbidden for US citizens to travel there in those years). When I returned I graduated from UC Berkeley, and completed graduate work in Journalism.

I was News Director at KPFA-FM in Berkeley in the

late 1960s/early 1970s, where I anchored daily newscasts, did interviews with many activists and authors, and produced documentaries, reporting on and reflecting the militant spirit of the times. Since mid-2010 I've been active in the Revolutionary Poets Brigade, an organization begun in San Francisco with chapters in other states and nations.

I had written to Lincoln to let him know of Martin – that, in a small gallery in Shanghai, someone was speaking well of his late stepmother and the work she did decades before. On 27 December, the same day I heard from Martin, I received an email back from Lincoln.

Date: Tue, 27 Dec 2011
Subject: Vicki

Dear Linda – thanks so much for your emails about Vicki. I did not get the first email or I would have responded right away. In any event, now we are in touch! …

For this email, I just wanted to let you know that I at long last got your email, as Claude Marks at Freedom Archives sent the email to me – I am a co-founder of the group and volunteer there frequently.

Several African-American academics in the US have done work related to Vicki since her death – I will send you that information as well as some other things that will interest you and Martin – she would be so happy to know that he and you have made this connection! I have never returned to China after my year there in 1965-6 tho my father and Vicki went back a number of times. I know it has changed hugely, and that's an understatement!

So, give me a couple weeks and I promise I'll get back to you in more detail about Vicki's life here after China, her memorial that my sister Miranda and I organized in New York, some photographs and related things. I have been meaning to put up a slide show about Vicki on the Freedom Archives website for some time – maybe this will help me move forward on that!

All the best and if you don't hear from me by mid-January, please don't hesitate to write again!

Lincoln

January came and went. I was busy preparing to leave for Paris, where I was scheduled to live till September. Preparations for yet another relocation overseas became so intense that I had little time to think about Vicki and Martin and the revolution that had brought them together. Secretly, though, I wished only to return to China, where I felt I had found something precious and rare, but which I also found hard to name.

It wasn't until more than a year later, in mid-February 2013, after my time in Paris, another city of revolutions, that I emailed Lincoln to remind him of his offer to send me further information about Vicki. I felt bad that I had kept Martin waiting so long. But perhaps after all this time, the decades of turmoil and revolutionary changes, waiting for one more year was a small challenge.

A couple of weeks later, I heard back from Lincoln.

Date: Sun, 3 Mar 2013
Subject: RE: Vicki

Hi Linda:

So sorry not to have gotten back in touch sooner, and appreciate the reminder!

If I didn't last time, I should mention this book, which has a chapter about Vicki by Dayo Gore, a scholar who I think is still working on more about Vicki.

It's called: *Want to Start a Revolution?: Radical Women in the Black Freedom Struggle.*

I recommend it!

Along with his email Lincoln sent a vivid collection of photographs of Vicki, from her teen years to old age. I forwarded it all to Martin, who replied swiftly:

Date: Mon, 4 Mar 2013
Subject: RE: about Vicki Garvin

Dear Linda,

I was always thinking of you after I received your latest email several month ago. I still remember that you told me you will stay in Paris for 6 months. Just 2-3 days ago, I think it is many months passed. Is it the right time you back to Australia? Thanks to God, your email with the photos of Vicki coming!

As I planned, I will decorate a special showcase in the Peace Gallery for my Teacher Garvin, with the photos you have sent me, with the text papers which I am keeping for 40 years, and other memorabilia. I will send you pictures of the showcase after it done.

Shanghai is in Spring now. The weather is always fine. Come back here if you have a chance. We are waiting for you!

Our correspondence was sporadic over the next few years, but Martin fulfilled his dream of commemorating Vicki at the Peace Hotel. I received his news via delightful emails.

Date: Sat, 6 Apr 2013
Subject: RE: about Vicki Garvin

Dear Linda,

Haven't heard from you for more then one month. May be you haven't got any information from Lincoln too.

But I have had already showing the memorabilias of Vicki Garvin in the display cabinet of Peace Gallery as I think of her.

I haven't use the images which you send me but I use one download from the website myself.

Here I attached the picture of the display cabinet for your information.

Kind Regards!

Martin Ma
Director of Peace Gallery

Date: Sun, 7 Apr 2013
Subject: RE: about Vicki Garvin

Dear Linda,

How a nice plan it is!

Everything is ok for me, I am ok with the idea of appearing on the radio documentary, I wouldn't mind you made it into a story for your next book and use the interview you record with me.

In the picture of the display cabinet of Vicki Garvin which I sent to you last email, the typed page is written on the English lessons of Quotations from Chairman Mao, which was used as the text book.

Here I attached some more of the English lessons text paper and other notes written by Vicki to me about the English classes at the time during the culture revolution.

And some word doc. from website for your reference.

With best wishes!

Martin Ma
Director of Peace Gallery

Date: Mon, 8 Apr 2013
Subject: RE: about Vicki Garvin

Hi again Linda,

We have published a book named 'Peace Impression' last year. And I am the one of the three writers of this book. There is a paragraph of Vicki Garvin. Now I give you the text as below for your information.

Tears of African American Teacher Vicki Garvin

In 1965 an African American woman Vicki Garvin arrived in Shanghai. Her Husband was a leader of the black liberation movement [whose members were] assassinated. And she too became a target. With the help of the friends, she was appointed as an English teacher in Shanghai International Studies College, during the Cultural Revolution, she had to move to Peace Hotel due to the fighting between school students. When she found that hotel staff spoke poor English, She offered to teach them English for free.

Garvin divided the hotel staff into elementary and medium classes. Lacking any textbooks Garvin taught the students using the English version of Quotation from Chairman Mao. Even the material in the hotel rooms were adapted for teaching. Those text books are kept by her students till today.

On April 4, 1968, the assassination of Martin Luther King shocked the whole world. On April 16, Mao Zedong made a public 'Declaration of Supporting African Americans' Resistance'. The fight of African Americans was never supported by their own politicians but supported by the great Chinese leader Chairman Mao, said Garvin when shedding tears.

Martin Ma
Director of Peace Gallery

*

For weeks after I arrived back in Brisbane I couldn't get the smell of Shanghai out of my things. After washing all my clothes it was still there. Was it in my skin, embedded in my hair, rubbed into my scalp? I washed some more, sprayed perfume, burned incense and fragrant oils.

After another week of sniffing, I realised the smell was coming from my laptop. But although I scrubbed and polished my computer till it sparkled, it still retained the distinctive smell of the city. I imagined that it had been created by pollution, multi-ethnic cooking, motorbike and car fumes, and the scent of millions of people – their wishes and their dreams, their smiles and their politeness, and their unassailable belief in an economic stability that would magically erase the sufferings of their past. Every time I opened my laptop to write about the city I could smell Shanghai – coming straight from my laptop's heart, I would joke to myself.

I can still smell it now.

But that wasn't all Shanghai had left me with. When I got back home, I was depressed for well over a month. I had initially thought it was a particularly awful case of jet lag, but after several more weeks passed I realised it was something deeper. A friend suggested to me that perhaps I was mourning.

Mourning for what? I asked.

I don't know, she replied. *Did you fall in love over there?*

Not with anyone in particular. Kind of with everybody I met though, I suppose.

Then you're in mourning for Shanghai. You miss it and your heart is a little broken.

I knew she was right. I had fallen in love with the city just as you would a person.

Maybe it's just the stimulation I miss, I suggested. *The excitement of feeling that you're at the new centre of the world. That feeling of foreignness that makes everything so ... new ... and fresh.*

That's what you live for, isn't it? she asked. *That foreignness. Some people dread it. But you love it.*

She knew me well. I loved every place I visited. But some perhaps more than others.

*

Date: Wed, 22 Apr 2015
Subject: A presentation of Vicki

Hi Linda,

I asked the Director of the Peace Museum, is the presentation of Vicki still exist in the Museum? She checked and sent me the photos by iPhone. I am trying to send it to you now.

Martin

Date: Fri, 24 Apr 2015
Subject: RE: A presentation of Vicki

thankyou so much for arranging to send these Martin

I am wondering how your life is? are you still working at the hotel?

How is Shanghai? I miss the city so much. I am still writing the story about Vicki!

warm regards
linda

Date: Sat, 9 May 2015
Subject: RE: A presentation of Vicki

Sorry for my late reply.

After three years worked as the Director of Peace Gallery, I had finally finished my work of 49 years and 10 months in the Peace Hotel in July, 2013. Now I am quite enjoying my retired life. For my son's family is staying with us, so I have to look after my grand-daughter, a 14 months baby girl after her parents going to work. I am quite busy helping my wife with her housework.

The elder school in my district ask me to teach Oral English from ABC for 30 old man students once a week. So I am a little busier.

Shanghai is not change too much recently, I think. Come again if you miss the city so much.

I am so interested you are still writing the story about Vicki. I would like tell you one more thing. There was a young lady who worked with Vicki in 1968 in Shanghai. She is an English woman about 30 years at the time. Her name is Knight. Once she asked me, what's your name? After I told her my name is Ma. She laughed and said, your name means a horse in Chinese. My name is knight, means a man ride on the horse. It's so funny, that's why I still remember her name so clear up to now.

Warm regards!

Martin

*

Recently, I dreamed I was in Shanghai again. That I walked into the lobby of the Peace Hotel, through which the sound of the guqin cascaded like a waterfall, and climbed the steps to the gallery, where Martin, with his dazzling smile, was waiting for me – not for me to return after my visit to Shanghai, but for me to arrive, decades after his country's last official revolution had ended.

The dream prompted me to go through the audio files I had stored on my laptop. After a couple of dead-end searches I came across a folder called 'Shanghai Sounds'. I opened it and spent a few hours listening to the recordings I had carried home with me as a memento of my visit.

I heard again the traffic zipping down Huichuan Road through Zhongshan Park; the Afghani music I would surreptitiously sway my hips to at the Uyghur Restaurant; the hair-raising taxi ride I took once through peak hour to get to a book event in the city's tourist precinct; the gorgeous kids at Starbucks and their *nihaos* to everyone who walked in through the doors; the flower lady outside the station; the announcements on the subway trains, made in perfect Chinese-accented English; the milling crowds along the Bund and the click and whir of a thousand phone cameras as they recorded this spectacular moment in their city's history.

The sounds conjured up Shanghai for me on the computer that still carried the faint scent of the city, and made me laugh and cry at the thought of what I had left behind. And, despite my promises to return when I left, I knew I might never see any of it again.

Finally, I came across the recordings I had made at the Peace Hotel. Of Martin and his smiling voice talking about the hotel's tumultuous history, about Vicki Garvin and the Cultural Revolution. Of Miriam plucking and strumming 'The Butterfly Lovers' at high tea and her description of how the lovers turned into butterflies so that they would never be apart. And I thought of how stories can be like butterflies too: transformed by longing into something delicate, beautiful and difficult to pin down.

Wild Strawberries in Mongolia

My sister packed tubs of fresh strawberries in our suitcases the morning we left for Ulaanbaatar. Cathie had heard there were shortages of many things in Mongolia's capital, and strawberries in particular were nearly impossible to get hold of. She was used to the variety of travel but these days she liked to know at least what she was having for breakfast. Hence, she had packed the strawberries, along with a carton of So Good soy milk and some Weet-Bix covered in Glad Wrap.

We were departing from Hong Kong, where Cathie was head of music at the Chinese International School. Unlike many of the expats she worked with, who lived on the main island of Hong Kong, she lived in Kowloon, where she bought Weet-Bix, So Good and most of her preferred Australian brands at the local supermarket. Things like her favourite bread mix were harder to find, but Cathie managed to get a steady supply from friends who'd visited her regularly since she'd relocated to Hong Kong.

She'd been at the school for a couple of years and I was on my first visit. I'd been invited to give some writing and songwriting workshops at the school, and to accompany a group of CIS students on one of their annual international field trips. These trips occurred in a school hiatus called Project Week, during which the students travelled to various parts of the world and performed civic-minded projects for those less fortunate than themselves. Knowing that most CIS students came from wealthy families, I imagined that many people in the world could qualify as less fortunate. In Cathie's opinion, though, Project Week was a good consciousness-raising opportunity for these kids, many of whom held multiple passports and expected to further their education at Harvard or Oxford.

Our group had elected to visit Mongolia and help the Christina Noble Children's Foundation. On the outskirts of Ulaanbaatar, the foundation had built the Blue Skies Ger Village for kids in need, and the CIS students would be donating and erecting a ger. A ger, or a yurt, is a demountable home that can be cooled in summer or insulated in the long harsh winters for which Mongolia is especially famous. I thought it was an ingenious design, perfectly suited to the nomadic animal herders of Mongolia, who travelled in search of pastures to feed their livestock.

I was going to Mongolia as an observer and archiver of the trip. I was also gathering material for a possible radio documentary. Consequently, on the morning my sister packed the fresh strawberries, I was more concerned that I had remembered all the equipment I needed: my recorder, a supply of discs and batteries, a microphone, and headphones.

I was more intrigued than worried about the trip, though I was quite prepared for most of my preconceptions to be overturned. I brushed up on my rudimentary Mongolian history – on Genghis Khan, for instance, who conquered Eurasia in the twelfth and thirteenth centuries, after leading his battalions of horsemen from the desert all the way east to Constantinople. He was also, I discovered, the hero of a 1950s film called *The Conqueror*, a schlock-fest starring John Wayne and produced by Howard Hughes. Did the maverick Hughes see himself, I wondered, in Genghis Khan? The Mongol leader was either reviled as a genocidal maniac or revered as a great nation builder – or, in the case of *The Conqueror*, 'loved by women, respected and feared by men, worshipped by his people', a rugged movie hero played with Fu Manchu moustache and leather breastplate by a notoriously right-wing American actor.

*

After travelling via Incheon airport in Seoul, we arrived at Ulaanbaatar early in the morning. As the plane taxied along the tarmac, I saw the name of Mongolia's main airport in giant letters across the top of the concrete terminal: *Chinggis Khaan International Airport*. I was surprised to see such public proof that Genghis Khan was idolised in the same way that John F Kennedy had been in the US – as a great historical figure and an inspiring leader. I pressed my nose against the plane window and peered further into the rolling fog, recalling what a Chinese acquaintance in Hong Kong had told me the night before.

The western view is never the complete view. When the west declines, their narratives will no longer dominate and a new, less incomplete history of the world will be written.

We left the plane, sleepy and dishevelled, and stumbled to the terminal through dispersing fog. At the transit centre we were processed by taciturn guards dressed in Russian-style military uniform, an unexpected juxtaposition of Asian heritage and European influence. The guards, both male and female, appeared severe and not exactly inclined to expedite our passage through immigration, despite the presence of twenty or so tired teenagers from Hong Kong. Finally, a bleary-eyed translator arrived, and by dawn we were bussing our way to the centre of the city.

The next surprise came when I opened the curtains of my room at the Lotus Hotel just past dawn. On the street, Soviet-style buildings fanned out like concrete blocks in a military compound; in the cold light they looked ominous, a flattened-down totalitarian's dream. It seemed another incongruous integration, a jolting reminder of Mongolia's twentieth-century history, its so-called Russian era.

I was sharing a room with Cathie, and equally incongruous as the impression of Moscow from our hotel was the breakfast we shared: Weet-Bix, So Good and a couple of freshly sliced strawberries. Cathie placed the rest of the strawberries in the bar fridge. We would have to ration them, we agreed, if they were to last for our stay. There was to be no sneaking of strawberries during the day or for late-night snacks – a few each per breakfast would see us through to our return to Hong Kong. In the drizzle that hung around outside, Ulaanbaatar did seem the kind of place where nothing fresh could possibly be found, where anything sweet and delicious would only exist in dreams or fables of other exotic lands, just as Mongolia existed in the dreams of faraway countries like Australia. Through the misty keyhole of Ulaanbaatar, my first impression of Mongolia was that of a harsh place, with a legacy of faded glories.

In the lobby, refreshed after a post-breakfast shower and nap, I met an Australian named Jack. In his cream jacket, blue trousers and scuffed brown shoes, he looked like he'd be at home at an RSL. But his cheerful face and bulging wallet told me he'd struck a deep vein of joy and profit here in Ulaanbaatar, and he laughed generously throughout our conversation at the hotel bar. Jack was working with an NGO facilitating mining projects in western

Mongolia. There were a lot of men and women like him in the country, he explained, from Australia, Canada and America, working at some vague consultancy job aimed at establishing mining ties with Mongolia. The country was eager, even desperate, for income with which to develop its nascent nationhood. As soon as the Russians had moved out, western companies had moved in. I would be told this several times during my visit, as if to confirm that the only alternative to the iron-fisted patronage of the Soviets was the velvet-gloved exploitation of the capitalists, who vigorously courted Mongolia as it opened up its economy.

It all felt faintly unseemly, the enthusiasm of business to 'help' Mongolia grow. Even Jack conceded this, as well as the need to 'tread carefully'. Mongolians, he sighed, were a proud people. Subsequently, there were already rumblings in the population, uneasy at how quickly the government had signed away its rights to the country's potentially enormous wealth. There was also talk of winding back some of the more outrageous and lopsided agreements with the western mining giants, with their deep caches of cash and expensive cadres of lawyers and experts.

I told Jack I was interested in discovering what I could about contemporary Mongolia, and in particular Ulaanbaatar. Jack gave me his card, telling me there were two English-speaking Mongolian women at his office who would be interesting for me to talk to.

You can read all you want about Genghis Khan and dream about the horsemen who made it all the way to Constantinople, he told me gruffly. *But a fascinating history won't feed the people of this country. You can understand that walking down any street in Ulaanbaatar. The things most people know about Mongolia happened nearly a thousand years ago. And all this place wants to do now – all it needs to do – is look forward, not backward, and grow. Grow up! And that's a whole other story. That's where we come in. When the Russians walked out the Mongolians needed someone to help them and that's what we're trying to do.*

When the Russians walked out. I wondered what exactly those words meant. I hoped someone would unpack the seemingly casual phrase for me before I left. How could a nation that had been so dominant in Mongolia simply walk out? What were the processes of their departure and what were its consequences?

*

When I am recording sound for a documentary, something transforming, and in some instances mysterious, takes place. Just as Christopher Isherwood became a camera in his Berlin stories, I feel I become something other than myself: a listening device through which pass information, emotion, exploration, conflict, colours, textures and light.

As I stamped along the footpath outside the Lotus Hotel that morning, waiting for the chartered bus to take our group to the city premises of the Blue Skies Ger Village Project, I could tell I would need extra focus in Ulaanbaatar. The city challenged and discombobulated me, and I would need to harness my strength to make sense of what I was witnessing. But I also felt, and hoped, that concentrating such energy here in Mongolia might reveal something unexpected, something clarifying, about not just the world but my world too.

When we got to the building, I set up my recording equipment and felt myself become that other me, the aural witness to an experience I would later re-stitch into sound montages. These montages might then make meaning from the fragments I carried home with me, these shards of Mongolian sound and light, embedded like jewels in my tiny discs.

The CIS kids gave out clothes and toys as I roamed the rooms and corridors, recording the sounds of this children's sanctuary. If the foundation's aim was to provide a feeling of safety to children who had never known such a thing in their lives, then Christina Noble and her team had succeeded. I was struck by the courage of this place, existing in this cold, difficult city.

The manager of the premises was a stocky nugget of an Irishman called Eoin, who knew Christina Noble from Dublin. He had spent time as an orphan on the streets, as she had, and believed passionately in her work. Sitting across his desk from me in his small, well-organised office, Eoin spoke candidly but guardedly, as if the obvious privilege of my life would make it impossible for me to relate to or empathise with the children in his care. I knew first-hand about first-world guilt: how it can create an intellectual understanding of an 'other' in relation to yourself, and at the same time a 'compassion disconnect' between you and the rest of the world. Sometimes there is simply no way to envision oneself in another person's circumstance – the imagination just can't travel that far.

I wondered if Eoin resented the time spent talking to someone like me. I imagined he had encountered a lot of people who were initially overcome by sympathy in Ulaanbaatar, but whose promises transformed into the embarrassed silence of unanswered emails and unfulfilled pledges when they returned home.

I had been one of those people and I knew how easily it happened. So I didn't make any promises that day. I just listened as energetically as I could to Eoin's words, admiring his tough, clipped sentences, his street-smart perspective, and the way he'd learned to trust action, not words, no matter how kind those words were. If Ulaanbaatar was one of the toughest places in the world to be an orphaned child, then he needed to be that tough too.

In between responding to numerous requests from his assistant, who popped in and out of his office as we spoke,

Eoin explained some key aspects of Christina Noble's philosophy and the specifics of his Ulaanbaatar experience. As he spoke in his deep staccato growl I could hear the children laughing. It wasn't broad or confident laughter; instead it was tentative, nervous. But it was laughter, nonetheless, or the manifest potential of it.

The CIS students were doing their best to get involved. They knew, though, that their own security would never be jeopardised in the way these children had been endangered all their lives. They knew that at the end of the day there was a bus to take them back to their hotel. They knew that when they had finished eating and playing and exchanging notes on the day's activities, they could take the lift up to their rooms, where freshly made beds waited to receive their weary bodies. But still, I thought, it wasn't meaningless that we were there. I refused to believe, in this courageous, unlikely place, that any act bringing two impossibly separated worlds together was futile. I listened again to the hopeful sounds of the Mongolian children at play. It might have been only a brief moment in our shared disparate histories, but it was at least something that we had made the long journey to arrive here.

Against this counterpoint of gentle, anomalous laughter, Eoin continued.

It's hard to believe they can laugh at all. But that's the miracle – the resilience of children. And we get kids from the worst of the worst, who've truly experienced the kind of hell you wouldn't even see in war zones. They have endured things you or I could not imagine. Some kids here were set alight by their parents because they couldn't afford to keep them. Other kids were put out of their homes when their mothers married again, and were left to cope on their own in the cold. For the sake of the new husband, all remnants of the first marriage had to be abandoned. It's a practice we are trying to gradually change, although the patriarchal nomadic life is deeply embedded into Mongolian culture and we have to tread carefully. That's why our Blue Skies Ger Village is central to our work for children in Ulaanbaatar. The bottom line, though, is that all those who are abandoned have a home with us. Of course, not every child wants the routine we set up at the orphanage. Some kids come here and leave. Run away.

Where do they go? I asked neutrally, not wanting to express any shock which might betray judgement.

The streets. The rubbish dumps. They work for scraps in the night markets. I mean, these people are tough, the toughest people on earth, I sometimes think. You've heard of the kids who live in the pipes under the streets? We run our mobile medical clinic for them at night.

I hadn't heard of them. These kids lived in gangs, going to and from their underworld through Ulaanbaatar's manholes. Eoin told me they'd been the subject of an international photographic exhibition; it had caused a recent media sensation, briefly focusing the world's attention – not always helpfully – on some of the worst of modern Mongolia.

Many of those kids spent some time here, Eoin further explained. *But they feel, for better or for worse, that they'd prefer to build their own community. To be independent. To move as they feel. Most of these people are descendants of nomads, of horse people who roamed the plains. So maybe they prefer it underground. Some of them have been there for years. We can't force them to do anything; all we can do is provide them with food or medical attention every night or whenever they need it. It's not our business to make judgements or to enforce our rules on them. But that's what I mean when I say they are tough.*

As he led me out of the building, he promised to arrange for me to go out one night with the mobile clinic, so I could see how the tunnel kids lived, and understand why they might prefer it over the care of government shelters or orphanages. The next night, I took him up on his offer and witnessed children ascending from beneath the earth for food and hot drink before descending into their homes under the streets. Others have written about these street kids in Ulaanbaatar after living with them over the course of weeks. So I'll leave it to their stories to illuminate the plight of these children, a plight I could barely understand or properly tell after two hours in the back of a mobile clinic.

*

Later that day I travelled with the CIS kids to the edge of the city. From its perimeter Ulaanbaatar looked as if it had been encircled by gers as part of some metaphorical encroaching of history. The nomadic homes seemed benign enough, with their colourful flags fluttering in the breeze. But their presence presented another incongruity of modern Mongolia: the nomads being transplanted into the city, their seasonally based lives taking on the rhythms of urban reality.

Mongolia seemed determined to preserve the heritage of its wandering tribes. But at what cost to the nomad, I wondered. The life they knew depended on constant movement, on harmonising with nature. How would they find a place in a new Mongolia, centralised in cities? How would the government legislate their position in relation to the oncoming mining boom?

That morning the name of the Blue Skies Ger Village was poignantly yet dazzlingly apt. The sky above us was the kind of cloudless blue you might dream up – crisp and so clear you could imagine it being peeled back like the top layer of a painting, revealing the workings of its creator's hand underneath.

Temujin was one of the young men from the foundation helping with the Blue Skies project. I guessed he was in his early twenties, and he had the face of a future leader. He already seemed compassionate and mature beyond his years as he surveyed the area around us. We stood together on a rocky incline looking over the spot where the ger was being assembled. I felt guilty not to be helping, but at that distance I had the luck to witness the process in its entirety. I could observe the CIS students' tentative attempts to get involved. I could see the equally tentative yet gentle way the Mongolian helpers showed them how to push up the ger's walls, how to install the vital layers of insulation, how to roll out the floors. Instructions were passed on almost inaudibly: it was a matter of showing and doing rather than telling.

Standing back as an observer also gave me a chance to talk to Temujin, who told me in halting yet clear English that he'd been born in the capital, and had lived there ever since. When I asked him if he minded me recording our talk, he only smiled and said he was a 'typical' Mongolian youth, proud of his country and its history. I tried not to show my surprise when he said he was only fifteen. This made him younger than many of the students I had accompanied to Ulaanbaatar. It was clear, though, that he had already endured a great many responsibilities, and he spoke with the thoughtfulness of a much older boy.

Yes, he told me shyly, his name was the same as that of the boy who grew up to be Genghis Khan. No, his parents hadn't named him that; he had chosen it for himself when he was ten in the hope that he would become a strong leader of Mongolia one day, as the original Temujin had been.

He had worked since he was twelve, while still attending school. As well as assisting at the ger village, he was studying computer programming four days a week and working as a delivery boy on weekends. He was also training to become a DJ, which gave him much happiness and a feeling of freedom. His favourite music was hip-hop and he practised spinning his records every night in one of the small clubs that apparently thrived in the city. I told him what I had told others since I had arrived: that Mongolia was full of surprises.

He talked about his plans as we watched the ger take shape. *Of course I want to go to America one day to study like my sister. She went to study politics.*

You want to live there eventually? I asked. *The home of hip-hop?*

If you don't mind me correcting you, he ventured shyly. *But to me and most of my Mongolian friends, hip-hop is a world language, not just American. And if I, or we, go to America, it is still our duty as young Mongolians only to study there, to study and learn as much as we can to help our country. We must return to build Mongolia. It used to be when my parents were students that most Mongolians who went abroad travelled to Moscow to study; the Russians were generous with scholarships and help with education. But when Russia couldn't do it anymore, America and other western countries offered to help. But you know it is always at a price. And we have to be careful we don't offer too much of ourselves in return for their help. We have to remain independent.*

I was moved at how articulate he was about his country, its recent past and its immediate future. I couldn't imagine boys back home feeling things so deeply. They would be channelling their energies into sport or computers, enjoying the freedoms of their boyhood, while their parents shouldered most of their burdens.

I asked Temujin what he felt about the Russians.

You'd think that we would hate the Russians, he mused. *I know that the Americans think we should. But my parents don't hate the Russians. They speak Russian. And in some way they miss the Russians.*

They miss the Russians? I asked, betraying my prejudices. *What do they think about all the monasteries destroyed and the monks killed?*

It was one of the first things that came up about Mongolia when researching the country's twentieth-century history in western sources: how the Russians killed more Buddhist monks and destroyed more monasteries than the Chinese were purported to have done in Tibet.

I don't really know, Temujin answered after a few moments. *Perhaps they believed what the Russians told them – that they were trying to modernise Mongolia, to stomp out the superstitious practices and the power of the religions. Which may not have been such a bad thing. People were so frightened of the spirit world that they couldn't make decisions for themselves. Science has got to be part of the equation even for us in Mongolia. But I know it wasn't only Buddhism* that the Russians tried to stamp out. *They also tried to wipe out shamanism and that's the religion my parents' ancestors practised.*

A couple of the Mongolian workers approached Temujin for advice on where to position the ger. The area that had been initially chosen was proving to be unsuitable and the ger would have to be moved a metre or two. He went back towards the construction site with them and was soon surrounded by a group of men, with whom he conversed animatedly in the melodic local language.

I imagined Temujin as a young Genghis Khan reborn into contemporary Mongolia, not to lead a group of men into battle and destruction, but to direct them to construction and charitable work. Times had changed, I thought, and young Temujin, with his hip-hop posse and his IT degree, would be the new warrior of Mongolia, adept with language and thinking, ready for the modern world.

After the new placement for the ger had been decided, he returned with a self-conscious smile.

And you? I asked, picking up our conversation. *What do you feel about religion?*

I don't practise any religion, he replied. *But I do believe in honouring our ancestors and our past as the shamans do. I think sometimes to look forward we have to look back. I don't mean to the Russians, although according to my parents it's thanks to them that we have a city like Ulaanbaatar with buildings and roads and transport. But further back to when we built our great empire. All the young people are doing now is trying to survive and build the country up again. We became very weak and broken, like an old diseased man. Now we have to get well again.*

I was hesitant to probe further. I felt a bit like the western companies in search of the riches that lay deep under Mongolian ground. I shouldn't dig too deep, or take too much, and instead honour what he had offered me freely without demanding more. But I couldn't help asking another question; I was curious as to how a Mongolian boy saw himself in today's world: as an Asian or a Eurasian. Did he feel more closely aligned with China or with Russia, or halfway between the two?

I know my parents – and me too – are more worried about China than Russia. China already has outer Mongolia and naturally assume they have a right to us too. Soon they will be in a position to do something about it. And like I said my parents feel grateful to the Russians for modernising Mongolia.

They think it was worth it?

He looked at the ger, then lifted his gaze to the hills around us and the rows of nomad homes dotting the ridges.

You know, he said, *we see the past differently to the westerners. We don't see the world divided that way. We see things in long interconnected streams, as part of nature, as part of the sky. The idea of division is a man-made concept. Here we are, Russians to our north and China to the south. We don't want to be their best friend perhaps, but we don't want to be their enemy either. Now the Americans want our coal and our riches under the ground but we don't want to be aligned with anybody. It is time for Mongolia to be strong again. To be respected and perhaps even a little feared ... just a little*, he laughed, *as it once was.*

I notice you see things differently here, I told him. *I got a surprise when I flew into Ulaanbaatar and saw the airport was named after Genghis Khan.*

To us he is a great leader and a god and it would be good if someone like that rose up again in Mongolia.

He turned to go. He'd been called away again. The workers were now stringing flags across the entrance of the demountable home and wanted him to participate in the traditional blessing. To call the spirits of the ancestors to bring good fortune to the ger and all those who would live in it. Afterwards, he would head back into town to go to class. And after that he might spin his records for the young, hip nightclub crowd.

Temujin shook my hand as he said goodbye.

You know even in China they worship the original Temujin as a saint. Yet I know to you he is a monster.

It wasn't the first time I had been chastised for not understanding that western narratives of history aren't the only ones, and that, as he said, there are many ways to tell the story of our collective past. I watched him walk away, a young man with a purpose in this vast country. To wait for a leader like Genghis Khan to return and make Mongolian men feel strong again. I wondered what a strong man would look like – or sound like – in contemporary Ulaanbaatar. Perhaps he wore hip-hop pants and carried a microphone and rapped about history while a boy like Temujin worked the turntables, a warrior of the nightclubs and back streets rather than a horseman of the wide plains.

After the ger was blessed, our group was taken on a tour of the Blue Skies village. Most of these gers housed groups of children. I felt like an intruder as the kids opened their school books for us to peruse. If they weren't staring at the floor, they smiled shyly as we chatted to them, and replied to our mimed questions with soft giggles. The children were all gorgeous and looked well fed. But their insecurity was apparent in their eyes, which darted uncertainly to their carers from time to time.

As the CIS students played with the Mongolian children, I walked along the ridge at the perimeter of the village. I encountered Rory, the school's science teacher, who had accompanied our group as a chaperone. We stood together for a while and surveyed the barren hills around us. Blades of grass, and even a few tiny pink flowers, peeked out from under small rocks and mounds. I noticed, suddenly, the absence of things growing.

It had been an eventful, emotional day and I felt overwhelmed by the country's landscape with its unimaginable winters, where the temperatures dropped to –30 and sometimes −40 degrees Celsius. This was the centre of one of the first and largest world empires. How would it survive as a newly lawless Russia and the growing might of China pressed in around it? And I continued to be haunted by another question: when modernity finally overtook Mongolia, where would be left for its nomads to go?

Rory was a tall, well-built Scottish man with wild white hair and beard – a mountain man himself. He had a pragmatic view of the world.

What is the meaning of Mongolia? I asked him, half joking.

You mean existentially? Or philosophically? He didn't seem surprised at all by my question.

I don't know what I mean, I conceded. *I guess you wonder how a country like this survives. I mean, nothing much seems to grow here at all.*

You talk like an Aussie, he laughed, *with your endless bright summers. You take for granted that places are fertile, that suns shine, that waves roll on beaches. I notice Aussies also sometimes don't see the meaning or value in darkness or sadness. In the northern hemisphere, we survived for centuries in the cold, the dark, the barren, the bleak and unsmiling.*

He spoke without rancour. I had noticed that too, the tyranny of smiling, of upbeat brightness in warm countries. I wondered whether our *giddays* and *bewdy mates* were sometimes received as an affront by those like Rory, who might read our cheer as a denial of other, equally valid things.

We fell silent and stamped in tandem. I could tell that Rory found the cold bracing while I found it, mostly, wearing.

So no, don't worry about Mongolia, he continued thoughtfully. *It's on the rise, no question. It's like nature. There are peaks and low points, deaths and resurrection. The Soviets brought infrastructure, and at the same time they destroyed the superstition that gave Mongolia its old shamanic spirit, but which also kept it what we in the west would call backward. It's always a push and pull between extremes until things settle in their balance. But, if you are asking the question from a geographical angle …?*

I was thrown by the passion of his answer. But I was also beginning to understand that this trip to Mongolia was going to continue to upend my preconceptions.

I guess that's what I mean … perhaps.

Then Mongolia has great meaning for the rest of the world. Especially for the hot countries. Even if nothing ever grew here, it would still play its vital role. Because the permafrost under the ground here is what's keeping the earth cool enough for our continued survival. Without the big barren freeze of Mongolia we'd all be burned out … literally.

We drove from the Blue Skies village to a boys' prison, where I interviewed a fifteen-year-old charged with murder. The CIS students then gave an impromptu concert for the inmates, who reciprocated with some traditional folk songs.

The jail was harsh: concrete floors, iron-bar windows and an absence of nature.

In the evening, we walked across from our hotel to a rundown building where a group of artists presented a cultural showcase. We sat enraptured as young men and women danced Cossack style while a young woman dressed in blue struck the guqin. Afterwards, Mongolian throat singers astounded us with their depth and sonorous dexterity. I was moved to tears. It seemed amazing that such talent and artistry could exist in these impecunious circumstances. But there it was: brilliant and surprising.

That evening, in our hotel room, I surreptitiously took three strawberries from the punnet my sister had left in the fridge. It was pure thievery, but I needed something sweet and succulent to balance out the drama of the day.

*

The schedule on our final day in Ulaanbaatar was as full as the others had been. But in the late afternoon I found time to catch a taxi to Jack's office, in an inner-city cul-de-sac. I wanted to meet the two colleagues he had recommended I speak to. They greeted me warmly and introduced themselves: Gerel, an elegant mature woman, had lived in Mongolia her whole life, while Sarnai, a vibrant, talkative young woman, had recently returned from post-graduate studies in the States. They both spoke impeccable

English. We discussed the problems of contemporary Mongolia – how to raise its GDP, how to negotiate a more equitable mining agreement with western companies – for a quarter of an hour or so before Gerel surprised me with a story that revealed exactly what it meant when the Russians left Mongolia.

I was working in a university in the west of Mongolia. Like many people of my generation, I had studied Russian literature, and I was a professor of that literature at the university. My husband also worked there and we had just had our first baby. I remember it was a bitter cold winter and we all relied on our central heating to stay alive. The day the Russians left, all the electricity was turned off, and the gas. Everything suddenly went cold and dead. And there I was, with a young baby, wondering how we would survive. I know the west regarded it as a liberation. But in those freezing days, for us it was a catastrophe. Literally everything shut down. And that was our freedom.

After Gerel finished this story, there was a long silence. Sarnai broke the quiet with a laugh and, in her deep melodious voice, said: *Freedom means many things.*

The clock was ticking loudly, and I realised I needed to start making my way back to the hotel. Our flight to Hong Kong was at midnight.

I thanked Gerel for sharing her stories. We hugged, though in reality we were still strangers. Sarnai offered to share a taxi into the city with me. *You haven't experienced*

*peak hour until you've experienced peak hour in Ulaanbaatar.
I'll get the driver to get a move on.*

As we waited for the cab, I told Sarnai how my sister
had packed fresh strawberries to take with us to Mongolia
because we had heard it was difficult to find fresh fruit.
In return, when we were huddled inside the taxi, Sarnai
told me about her own family, who remained practising
shamans after years of being outlawed, persecuted and even
killed during the Soviet era. *It's in our blood*, she said. *And
what's in the blood can't be easily destroyed.*

But you are wrong about the strawberries, she continued,
as the car zigzagged through the twilight chaos of
Ulaanbaatar's peak-hour traffic. *If you go up in the hills,
just before spring, you'll find the richest, sweetest strawberries growing in the wild by the mountain streams. It's a
very clear sign to every Mongolian who understands nature.
Those wild strawberries tell us that the harsh winter is slowly
coming to an end, that the ice will thaw and flowers will
bloom again. You'll never taste anything like those wild
strawberries. They don't sell them in shops. They don't export
them to places in need of sweet fruit. But they are there, and
a Mongolian wild strawberry is the juiciest you'll ever taste.*
She laughed, abundant with the joy of her story, imagining perhaps that we were sharing those wild things in
the back of the taxi.

The CIS kids sang all the way to the airport that night.
I sat at the front next to Cathie and pressed my face up

close to the window so I could see the shapes and silhouettes of the city we were leaving as we passed into the night. I felt the enormity of the city's story, the magnificence of the country's heritage, and the bitterness of its loss. I also felt the hope of its future and the echoes of the hundreds of amazing stories it would tell.

Garbo Laughs in Paris

The distance between the two banks of Tallebudgera Creek was not insurmountable. But it still took me a number of years, from the time I was about eight to when I was nearly twelve, to finally cross it.

My father had taught us all to swim. He believed, I think, not just in the physical act of swimming but in its meaning as well. Although I had been determined to cross Tallebudgera Creek unaided like my father – who swam with only a pair of dark blue speedos and slatherings of zinc cream – I often wore snorkels, large goggles and a pair of flippers. My father was teasing when he said I looked like an alien stick insect, but as I glided across the top of the water, inspecting through my goggles the green-blue world below the surface, I felt as if I truly was an amphibious explorer from outer space.

Tiny golden red guppies swam past me; below, seaweed swayed like reed-thin performance artists with wildly flexible joints and an absence of bone.

I still have the piece of paper on which I wrote those words for a school essay. As a child I often experimented and over-reached with language, and I remember the exhilaration of making up phrases while in the water. Words were sensual, visceral, experiential – *wet like the creek, warmed in globular sunlight.* Despite my ambition, though, I would never dare to use such words when I described the crossing to Dad. He may have physically demonstrated his technique while teaching us to swim, but he also often talked in cryptic ways about the importance of balancing yourself in the water, of understanding the importance of graceful, regular movements and finding a symmetry between the rhythms of the arms and the feet. I don't know if he would have supported my exaggerated imaginings of the world beneath my gliding, gangly body. For him, the aesthetics and the form of a thing always seemed more important than its emotion and passion, which for me were primary. Still, despite the clumsiness of my efforts – in both swimming and using words – the swim was a high for me. After that summer, things changed and such primal achievements became less meaningful.

The year I crossed Tallebudgera Creek was also the year I got my first, and worst, case of sunburn. It was the result of lingering too long in the water, dreaming of the darkness underneath. *Whites like us aren't made for the sun*, my fair-haired, porcelain-skinned mother often admonished me. Nevertheless, as we approached teenage-hood, many of us persisted in that hopeless quest of getting a tan. My friend Helen Myerstown slathered cooking oil all over her skin before sunbaking one summer, thinking the subsequent burning would provide the illusion that her oddly shaped freckles had joined together to make her the right shade of brown. Instead she turned so red she had to be rushed to emergency, where she was lectured by several doctors about skin cancer. *We live in a country where the sun can kill you. And that's a fact*, the doctor told Helen. *That is a fact.*

Facts were supposed to protect us from the perils of the weather. So were the layers of zinc cream my mother rubbed across my back, as well as my face and shoulders, whenever we went to the beach after my bad sunburn. In the days and nights after the incident, I hadn't slept much. Mum had stayed up with me, pressing cold packs onto my back. As she tut-tutted about me learning my lesson, I lay curled up on my side, oblivious to potential scarring, a foetal Proust, before I knew who or what Proust was, remembering, as if I were an old man and not a young girl, days long past. And even though I was only eleven and a half and had never been kissed or held by a lover or suffered through unrequited – or requited – love, in my feverish delirium I knew I had already experienced physical ecstasy and done amazing things: like snorkelling from one white stretch of sand to another; contemplating the unknown things on the bed of a river that both spills out into and receives the sea; walking barefoot along the beach in my favourite leopard-print one-piece swimsuit, collecting shells and stones that I imagined had been thrown up on the sand at my feet for strictly metaphorical reasons. I believed then in messages, as well as facts. But I kept their meaning to myself.

*

I spent what I call 'my first winter in Paris' living in a small studio at the Cité Internationale des Arts in Rue Geoffroy-l'Asnier right by the Mémorial de la Shoah. The main entrance to the Cité on Rue de l'Hôtel de Ville is just across from Pont Marie, which is said to be the most romantic bridge in the world. Lovers from all over the globe converge on or near the bridge, most popularly at twilight, for kisses and embraces and sweet murmurings of eternal love.

I say I had my first winter, but for the most part it was spring. That year, March and April were unseasonably cold and wet, even for the Parisians, who loved to complain about the weather. For a Queenslander with a history of sunstroke and long Christmas holidays baking in the heat, it felt like the worst winter I had ever known.

I'd arrived in late February having been delayed by work in Australia. That was my official explanation anyway. It was true, but there was also an unofficial reason: my irrational fear of the cold. I had discussed this fear at length with my Parisian friend Marie, who assured me that I would adapt and cope by eating heavier food and dressing in layers. She advised me to invest in a good woollen coat, a pair of waterproof boots and a nice scarf and hat that I could put on and take off easily, as I would be moving regularly from the heated indoors to a sometimes bleak outdoors. The rituals for coping with cold weather seemed complicated and daunting, not to mention pricey.

Of course, the opportunity to live and work in Paris for six months made my fear seem embarrassingly trivial. But as I had neither experience nor facts to fortify myself with, I was anxious of what the cold might do to my body and psyche. The cold remained an ominous mystery for which no layers of attire or understanding could prepare me.

Contrary to my fears, the weather was surprisingly balmy during my first week in Paris. I was able to get through my jet lag and gradually establish a routine. During the first few weeks in a new place I try to orientate myself in the local area, and in Paris I established a walking route from the Cité to the Mémorial de la Shoah up to Rue de Rivoli, then left along to Rue des Archives where, after a couple of blocks, I would buy *The Times* and the *International Herald Tribune* from the Agora newsagent. I would then walk a few metres back down towards the Hôtel de Ville, and end up in Starbucks, where I would order a tea latte and read the day's news. The pleasure of reading a newspaper was something I rediscovered during my time in Paris.

The second day I walked along this route, it was very early, and when I got to Starbucks there were plenty of seats near the window, where I could read in natural light. A young woman sat down opposite me and opened her computer. I returned her smile – out of courtesy, but also out of delight at observing that she looked a lot like Marie, who also had long black curls, fair skin and penetrating but gentle eyes.

I smiled again and asked in my rudimentary French: *Ça va?*

Ça va et vous?

And so our conversation, which continued for over an hour and two cups of my favourite Earl Grey latte, began.

Mathilde studied Fine Arts and worked part-time at the Louvre. The thing she first divulged to me was her outrage at being approached that morning for a threesome with a man and his wife, just down Rue des Archives on her way to Starbucks.

So typical of Paris, she harrumphed. *It's no wonder we Parisian girls have a reputation for not smiling. Why should we give our smiles away for free? Here in Paris a smile is an invitation so we learn to keep our heads – and our mouths – down.*

I thought of similar conversations I'd had with Marie, who'd also told me of her relief, upon arriving in Australia, that smiles were given and accepted freely without hidden meaning or immediate sexualising. The freedom to smile was radical, she said. Her face had changed through the release of her smile; it not only liberated her mouth, lips and teeth, but exercised the muscles in her cheeks, and widened and lifted her eyes as well. It also gave her more courage – or was it also freedom? – to meet the eyes of another. After a year of smiling, her face had changed shape in the same way a body might after exercise. It was reformed physically and reborn philosophically.

I remembered, too, my mother's decoding of a smile and its meaning, contained in the advice she often repeated to her students as well as to her friends and children: *Smile and the world smiles with you.* Or in the famous Charlie Chaplin song about smiling through heartache, which she had once sung with breaking voice after her mother died. She believed in staying positive, and saw it as a corrective to my propensity for drama and tears.

But what if a smile became impossible? Or dangerous? Or subversive? What songs would be written, or sung, memorialised or remembered in a Parisian coffee shop then?

These questions occupied me only briefly; as far as I was concerned, my smile would never be threatened. It was still something I took for granted, an innocent part of my exchange with the beautiful Mathilde.

Our talk ranged over a variety of topics – Paris, the world, the history of painting, Starbucks, sex, shopping, the upcoming election – and ended in her offer to take me on a private tour of the Louvre at twilight, after the tourists had dispersed for the day. Even more significantly, though, she told me about the Forum des Images, the cinema archive centre in the heart of Les Halles. We had been discussing things to do in the cold, when the wind and rain might make it impossible to walk the streets or spend any time outdoors. Mathilde suggested I do what she did: spend the bleakest days at the Forum, where a ticket cost only five euros and where, if you had the time and the desire, you could educate yourself in the entire history of world film.

Later that day, I looked up the website for the Forum. Like many French sites, the pages looked at first to be overloaded with information. After a frustrating hour or so, I began to understand not only the idiosyncratic precision with which the site's information had been catalogued, but also how the Forum presented its films – usually in seasons with a common theme. There were, for instance, films about the forest, about the wild, about the war, about royalty; films from the New Wave, or literary adaptations.

Despite my best intentions, I didn't make it to the Forum in March, or even April. I was spectacularly derailed by both the weather and a bout of terrible insomnia that kept me up for nights at a stretch – I often felt I would fall over with fatigue. Defeated, I withdrew into my small, centrally heated room, and hibernated in the dark – *like a bear*, I wrote in emails home. For the first time I experienced what winter in the northern hemisphere might mean to someone raised in Australia.

Memories of summer became my consolation as I struggled through the cold days and even colder sleepless nights. This was ironic, considering how extreme I had always found the Queensland heat, how much I longed for coolness when I was sweltering through an Australian summer. In the lingering remains of a Parisian winter, remembering heat became almost Proustian. I lay in bed propped up under blankets and recollected a golden age – literally – of summers that warmed my fair skin and encouraged smiles on my freckled face. My memories, like this city, were rendered into poetic, beautiful fragments: pristine, static, inflexible to reinterpretation. The imagined narratives of my history became my defence against the cold and, like Balzac and Proust, I began to scribble them down in the dim light of my atelier.

I omitted all references to sunburn, the grit of sand in my shoes, the burning bitumen under my thonged feet. I didn't mention the mosquitoes drawing my blood as I tossed and turned under nets with holes big enough to allow squadrons of insects through.

Writing lit a fire inside me. When the central heating was switched off at midnight I warmed myself with reveries of Australian summers. By staying in my room so much, however, I became even more frightened of the cold. When I did go out I sucked in my chest and bent my body over, like an old woman, to protect myself in the wind. I hid my mouth and its smile under thick wool, and my bleary eyes peered out from the furry overhang of my Russian-style hat, the kind that bear hunters wear in the snow. In my struggle with the cold, I became displaced, in body, in thought, in emotion, in action – alien to myself, to everyone who knew me and even, I imagined, to the strangers who passed me in the street.

After a month or so of bending over and stomping and complaining about the cold, I noticed with alarm a gradual change to my face. Just as I had witnessed Marie's transformation by smiling, I saw my face change by not smiling. If a face contains a history of all the smiles that have radiated from it, the absence of smiles wipes something from it. That facial history chronicles periods of stasis and development, of strife and prosperity, of peace and war. After I saw my sinking mouth in the mirror, I would sometimes imagine, in my addled, wakeful dreaming, that a kind of darkness was falling on a great civilisation.

I began to understand I was depressed that April in Paris. All the songs, the films, the myths, the dreams – not to mention the expectations of my envious friends back home – had told me I should be shopping on the Champs-Élysées, sipping coffee and discussing life at Les Philosophes café in the Marais, or strolling through twilight arm in arm with an older lover across Pont Marie. But I was maudlin and depressed. And because this was Paris, the city of love, where only an exile from the human race could feel down, I felt like a failure. Still, gloom doesn't always pick its moment – or at least you can't pick gloom's descent. I was alone, sleepless and cold, and instead of taking medication to lift my spirits I dreamed of swimming in the Gold Coast waters and feeling sunburn on my back.

As my face changed, I searched for answers in my own history that might give some clue as to why I had so quickly surrendered to the dark forces of the weather. Peering into the lines that the cold had carved around my eyes, I became focused on a particular period of my history, which was also to do with a face. Not mine, but another face that rarely smiled.

That face belonged to Greta Garbo, with whom I became obsessed when I was eleven, the same year I crossed Tallebudgera Creek. It was a long, difficult year, an age when new obsessions would energise me. I first encountered her face in a library book, a large hardback printed in black and white. Its title was *A Pictorial History of the Movies* and it offered readers hundreds of glamour shots and stills from movies, dating from the silent beginnings of American cinema. (They didn't think to include the films of the French, though, who told me frequently, and ruefully, how they invented cinema as an artform long before Hollywood made a business out of it.)

The cinema section at our local library consisted of a seemingly random collection of books. I didn't care whether the books were scholarly or trashy, erudite or populist. I devoured them all. Reading about films satisfied not only my attraction to the mystique and glamour of cinema, but also my curiosity about words and ideas, which often seemed to me as exotic as creatures of the deep might appear to a landlocked person. But it was the images of Garbo, mostly in black and white, that entered my dream consciousness and touched what I imagined in those days was my soul.

Greta Garbo seemed to be everything I was not, the unimaginable other to my pre-adolescent self: the angled to my round, the exotic to my plain, the profoundly silent to my chatty. While I lived in harsh sunlight, she inhabited an alien, black-and-white world of shadows, as if she were in a dream, or had just been roused from a deep sleep. I was too awake. I was already suffering from the insomnia that would plague me years later in Paris. Instead of sleeping, I read books and dreamed my way into another life. And while it was my mother's and grandmother's mantra to keep busy through all of life's ups and downs – for otherwise the devil might do his work – Greta seemed above this. It was as if she had arrived having completed all her tasks, as if the effort required for *doing* had ended and *being*, in all its fullness, had become possible. There was nothing of the devil's work in or around her.

In summer, when the heat turned my mother's face bright red, she would mutter, *Oh hell*. My face became splotched with red too: we were incongruously coloured for our weather. Though we burned and fretted in summer, we never thought to move back to the part of the world where Greta came from. Looking into her face, rendered inertly in monochrome, I felt the possibility of coolness, of silence and peace.

Though the world referred to her as Garbo, to me she was always Greta, a name that made her seem more capable of the quiet conversations I craved with her. I wanted more than just to stare at her face in a book: I wanted to relate, to know, to understand. If I could have moved her by magic, I would have wished her to step off the page and into my life, to teach me stillness in a world of incessant noise and movement.

I devoured as much information as I could about her. I discovered that she and I were descended from the same Scandinavian tribe: my great-grandfather was born in Stockholm, where Greta had grown up as Greta Lovisa Gustafsson in the early years of the twentieth century. I also learned that when she first arrived in Hollywood she was a plump, sullen girl with frizzy hair and crooked teeth – her looks were overhauled by her bosses at the studio, but her essence, that ineffable something which Bette Davis called 'witchcraft', was already there, all hers.

There was a picture in a book called *The Allure of Garbo* that illuminated the difference between Swedish Greta and Hollywood Greta, a transformation that seemed impossible. I looked into the mirror and wondered how puffy rosy cheeks could ever hollow out into contoured angles – I practised sucking in my cheeks, but that only made my mouth look like some weird fish. I tried to flatten down my unruly curls, but they sprang back up. Most difficult of all was trying to teach myself to look blank, and not to smile. It seemed unnatural to train my muscles to come to rest instead of cracking and creasing into all kinds of emotion. If Greta was the Swedish sphinx, I was more like a cartoon clown, Shirley Temple rather than Garbo.

I didn't glide or soothe or stare in silence at some unfathomable distance, like Greta does at the end of *Queen Christina* in one of her, and cinema's, most iconic images. I clanged and rattled around the world, and my father liked to tease me with the nickname Ding Dong: a bell that never stopped ringing, a brain that never stopped thinking, a face that never stopped moving.

Searching for more information, I had found *The Allure of Garbo* in the library. Although the sound of the word *allure* already suggested something mysterious and luxurious, I checked the dictionary for clarity. I found two definitions: 'attraction or attractiveness' and 'the quality of arousing interest'. The second definition seemed more appropriate – I wasn't aware of her attractiveness, as it might be perceived by a grown-up; sex had nothing to do with it. Her face aroused in me a curiosity for life, for stories, for mysteries that might be solved. Her face made me want to see.

The secret of Greta's fascination seemed to be that she didn't smile. Her face was at rest, undisturbed, her thoughts hidden. Sometimes I felt she was teaching me something significant, something that would take me many years to fully understand.

I imagined my mother – exasperated by such impassivity, which offered up nothing to organise, to mould, to train – telling Greta to cheer up, to keep smiling. And then I imagined Greta, my gorgeous guru, staring past Mum into the distance, refusing to react, in what one enraptured film reviewer called 'eternal self-possession'.

*

From May to July of 2012, the Forum des Images presented a season of Hollywood films that featured Paris. The eclectic program for *Paris vu par Hollywood* ranged from DW Griffith's 1916 classic *Broken Blossoms* to Woody Allen's recent commercial hit *Midnight in Paris*. It also included two of Greta's films: *Camille* and *Ninotchka*.

Camille, known in French as *Le roman de Marguerite Gautier*, was directed by George Cukor in 1936. The film was based on a novel by Alexandre Dumas, who had also adapted his book into a very successful play – its 1852 premiere at Théâtre du Vaudeville in Paris met with such acclaim that Verdi turned it into one of his most famous operas, *La Traviata*.

Camille was the film through which my obsession with Greta's face intersected with my mother's love of old romantic films. One steamy Sunday, I was reading, or staring at, *The Allure of Garbo* when Mum called me to join her in the lounge room. This invitation was a significant ritual of my childhood: my mother and I would watch a film, while my father absented himself in favour of lawn-mowing duties, or other serious things – reading Keats or Wordsworth, preparing for his lectures on Shakespeare, or solving the *Australian* cryptic crossword.

That afternoon, as we watched *Camille* on the television, my still, silent image of Greta became animated for the first time. During the opening titles, Mum whispered to me: *She was so beautiful. But, dear Lord, so was he.*

'He' was Robert Taylor, the dark-haired American actor who played Armand, Marguerite's younger lover, a character based on Alexandre Dumas.

They called his face the most perfect profile on earth, she continued, as if she were divulging something culturally important.

Mum always liked pretty men; she noticed their curling eyelashes, their cherub lips, their lovely skin, their beautifully manicured hands. For me, though, old-time movie actors were of little interest – I used to tell her it was because they wore their pants way too high. In fact, it was the women who attracted me in these old films: Garbo, Dietrich, Stanwyck, Crawford, Davis and Leigh. Mum would reel off their first names like they belonged to members of a local netball team – Marlene, Babs, Joanie, Bette and Viv – but she always referred to Greta as 'the divine Garbo'. I loved their glamour in the smoky absence of colour, the lack of sunlight in their worlds, the filtering out of anything too stark or too bright. Queensland was certainly too bright: sometimes even our brains felt cluttered by fire.

That Sunday was what Mum liked to refer to as 'another stinking hot one', for which, as usual, we were inadequately prepared. She fanned herself with an old plastic fan, which was gold with red tassels – it was from her days on the stage, used as a prop in *The Mikado*. I remember this motion clearly because, at that precise moment, Greta was also fanning herself on screen. My rapture at watching Greta was momentarily diverted by the tandem fanning of these two women, who had such an impact on my life, despite being vastly different.

When I later came to understand what *Camille* was about, I was amused that my conservative Catholic mother would have been so enthusiastic about the story of a high-class prostitute and her various lovers. But that also was the allure of Garbo and the fantasy of a black-and-white romance. I imagined that Greta's self-possession helped her transcend the roles in which she was cast: a temptress, a spy, a prostitute, a drunkard, a woman of loose morals, a great artiste, a sinner, a saint. Anyone but someone ordinary – she would never, for instance, play a suburban housewife like my mother.

Perhaps Greta was also the other for Mum: not the impossible other as she was for me, my opposite in every way, but the permissible other, who would be forgiven everything. And perhaps she even understood Garbo's appeal to her strange, awkward daughter: a woman standing outside normal codes, outside culture itself, emanating a kind of freedom to those who wanted, or needed, to see such things within her cool beauty.

In between sips of orange cordial, and the Iced Vo-Vos that Mum opened on special occasions, I observed an anomaly. Despite the subtle quicksilver movements of Greta's face, it seemed perfectly at rest, as if the emotional narrative of life was only a projection, and behind it her inner being was full of peace. I was mesmerised by the sense that in the maelstrom of a full and difficult life she was relaxed. Even though I didn't have the language for it at the time, I felt instinctively that I was witnessing a philosophy – that she had worked out how to move through the world by embracing rather than shunning the negative.

This especially appealed to me in the bright Australian space I inhabited, which insisted on positivity, on keeping one's spirits up, on showing the world one's bravest face. It was as if Greta was preparing me practically, realistically, for life. I wanted to be able to veil myself too. To be able to find what I thought I saw in her face: the aloneness that would protect me, that meant I could not be touched, until I chose, until I desired, to be touched.

*

During those cold months in Paris, I pondered what it meant to be unable to smile. When I was twelve and enamoured of Greta, when I wanted to have the choice not to smile if I didn't feel like it, I had never considered that you could take that ability for granted – or the way a smile could connect people.

I have formed friendships on the basis of a smile exchanged on the street. I met one of my longstanding friends along Boulevard de Sébastopol in 2005, just down the road from where I was living in 2012. In Paris, my smile said *oui*: it encouraged a smile from another; it invited a *oui* in return. As an Australian woman it seemed perfectly normal to celebrate a warm summer afternoon by smiling at a stranger in the street – I thought nothing more of it. An hour later, at a gig in Les Halles, I encountered him again: this time our smiles were of surprise. We kept running into each other that evening – on the stairs, at the bar. When at last we found ourselves on the street outside, we agreed to do more than just smile at each other in passing. Those smiling *ouis* had connected us, and eventually turned into laughs as we went back into the bar.

It was your smile that made me notice you, my friend told me later. *Women in Paris don't smile like that.*

I could tell you the story of what happened later, the things shared, offered and received. But I won't. All I will say for now, for purely anthropological reasons, is that a simple smile can lead to so much more, and that years later we still exchange emails and meet in Paris when we are there at the same time. A smile has its own language: it can whisper and shout and invite and sing. But it also lights up a face and opens up a space between people, where one can approach and be approached by another.

A few years before that first trip to Paris, I witnessed my mother's face frozen because of Parkinson's disease, an illness that would gradually make her whole body rigid. I had observed how her inability to smile signalled a threat to her existence as she knew it. But it was only when I myself couldn't smile, during my winter in Paris, that I understood her anguish at watching that light fade, that space narrow, that approach from and to others grow impossible. And I also understood, with an ache, why, when I was eleven and tried to veil my feelings like Greta did, my mother went to battle for my smile; why she exhorted me to keep smiling, when it was still possible to do so.

*

Another reason I had decided not to smile when I was eleven was my teeth. I had realised that the two tiny incisors on either side of my front teeth, which had been called my 'baby teeth' for years after I was no longer a baby, were never going to miraculously straighten or grow any longer to match the rest of my teeth. In photographs where I opened my mouth to smile, my teeth looked misshapen and awful. 'Little wolves' teeth' is how my elegant Aunt Lal had described them with mocking affection. Mum and Dad would never have dreamed of getting my teeth fixed, though. Not just because they didn't have the money, but because you accepted what the good Lord gave you and that was that. That was certainly that as far as my smiling in photos went. If I did have wolves' teeth, I was going to keep them to myself, as Greta had taught me it was possible to do: even though she had tiny, perfect teeth, she seldom showed them.

If I was a wolf in private, though, I wanted to show the world I could also come in from the wild. One afternoon, while Mum was in the kitchen cooking and probably singing, I crept into her room, opened the top right-hand drawer of her dresser and grabbed the first lipstick I could find. It was called 'A Coral Smile'. I also took the small hand-held mirror in which Mum sometimes checked the back of her curly head before going out. As a sudden last-minute inspiration I also snatched a tin of talcum powder. I stuffed everything into the waistband of my shorts before sneaking out the verandah door on my way to the back-yard, where I hoped to find that most unusual thing in our loud, rumbustious household: some privacy.

My stolen goods would take care of my face. What to do with my curls was another matter. Aunt Lal, who once tried to tame them with hairspray, said my curls had a mind of their own. I knew that sometimes my father flattened down his hair with something called Brylcreem. Knowing he kept his Brylcreem in the makeshift downstairs bath-room, I tiptoed there and discovered the small zipped bag in which it was always kept. I had a fleeting thought about how predictable my father's life was as I rifled through the bag's contents: a rusty razor, a toothbrush, a half-empty tub of Brylcreem. But I didn't dwell on it, the fact that he possessed so little, that he had given everything he had to the family, to us.

Next to the Brylcreem, I found a small jar of Vaseline, which I quickly purloined as well. I didn't know if people used Vaseline on their hair, but it looked, and smelled, strong enough to do the job.

Juggling all the things I had stolen close to my chest, I sneaked down the side of the house, sat beside the big banana tree at the back and got to work. First, I smeared the coral lipstick across my lips, pulled my hair back from my face and turned to the side to check out my profile in the mirror. My full cheeks looked like moons, but there was nothing I could do about them. They were my genetic curse, or blessing, depending on whom you were talking to. They would always make me look wholesome and un-mysterious, no matter what I did. But I would change what I could. Copying what I'd seen my mother do on many occasions, I dabbed some of the coral lipstick below the corners of my eyes: the spot where Greta's cheekbones were visible in most of her photographs. I dabbed and patted until I had created what I thought was a subtle, smudged texture, making the illusion of cheekbones where there were none.

Next, I damped down my hair and pinned it flat to my scalp with globs of Vaseline. This was relatively easy to do. The hardest part about taming my hair, I discovered, was dealing with the bits of frizz that framed my face like some kind of wiry halo. After much pulling and scraping and pressing, these rebellious hairs were stuck to my scalp, along with the rest of my curls.

I then tackled the problem of my skin, which was pink and blotchy from all my squinting into the sun. My eyes also bore the faint indents of goggles, like pale bruises. All I had to cover these imperfections were Dad's Brylcreem and Mum's talcum powder. It seemed a stroke of symbiotic genius when I decided to mix the two together so I could smear it, like Mum's Max Factor foundation, from their 'Make-up to the Stars' range, across my face.

Carefully, though with what I imagined was the diligent zeal of a research scientist, I placed the upturned Brylcreem lid on the grass, daubed some white cream into it, sprinkled talc over the top and then mixed it together. Against the bright summer grass of our lawn, the resulting concoction looked disarmingly unnatural. By that point, though, I was spurred on by a feverish obsession to see if I could become not just like Greta, but like 'Something Else', something outside the reality of myself.

With the mirror in one hand, I dabbed the mixture onto my skin – lightly at first, then more recklessly, hoping to produce the same magic in a Brisbane backyard that had been created on Greta decades earlier in a photographer's studio somewhere in Hollywood. It was, of course, a disaster. But at the time, like so many things during that year, it felt like a triumph.

At the end of the process, I looked again into the mirror. With my gleaming slicked-back hair, white moon face, coral lips and smeared cheekbones, I hardly looked human. I was a creature, just like Greta, without biological origins, who could not be defined or corralled as anybody's something. I was no longer my parents' daughter, with a crooked smile, curly-whirly hair and blotchy skin. I was the other that was me. Or so I imagined.

My mother saw me – and reality – before my father did. She spied me through the window at the back of the house. After alternately laughing and being aghast, a confusion that reflected what I had tried to accomplish that day, she proceeded to yell at me as she ran along the side of the house to where I was grinning with glee. She smacked me a few times, hard, on the bottom, and told me to get over myself while, at the same time, warning me not to let my father see me like this. Somewhere underneath all her outrage, I could hear her humour, as if she understood the absurdity of what I was trying to achieve, and how such a seemingly ordinary woman, which was always how she liked to describe herself, could have produced a daughter who looked like I did that day. Dad, on the other hand, just gave me a mock-withering look (perhaps he was amused too) when he joined us in the backyard, and told me to get that muck off my face before dinnertime.

I did neither. Not immediately. I barricaded myself in my room while they took turns telling me to let them in or, alternatively, to come out. I wasn't ready to do either. Not until I'd had the chance to hold up Greta's photograph next to my face and scrutinise our shared reflection in the mirror. It didn't make much difference to me that I saw exactly what my parents saw – a grotesque, clown-like version of my old self. Within that grotesqueness I saw the possibility of something. Even if it was only for the worse, I had for the first time taken the steps needed to transform myself.

Getting rid of what Mum called my 'ridiculous get-up' wasn't so simple though. A jar of her Ponds Cold Cream was all that was needed to wipe my skin completely clean. But no matter how much she rinsed my hair under the shower, no matter how she yanked and pulled, we could not scrape all the Vaseline out of my curls. In a last-gasp attempt at reasserting her practicality, she took the pair of sewing scissors from the bathroom cabinet, said to me, not unkindly, *Well, if you want a change I can help you*, and proceeded to chop off all the bits of hair that she couldn't scrub clean. In less than ten minutes of her barbering, most of my hair was gone. What was left looked like a frizzy swimming cap pulled down severely around my skull.

I would have been more shocked had Mum not already told me that she planned to get my hair cut short before school started again at the beginning of the upcoming year. Life was going to get more complicated: I'd have to get up earlier; I'd have to learn to become more organised. And, as Mum informed me, there certainly wouldn't be time anymore to take care of curls, especially the kind my grandmother wore when she was a little girl. My mother may have cut my hair to make a point. But it was destined to be shed anyway, along with so many other things that year.

*

The other film of Greta's that was showing at the Forum des Images was *Ninotchka*. It was first released in 1939, a golden year for films. Historians refer to it as 'landmark', 'momentous', 'outstanding' and 'the greatest single year in the history of cinema' both in terms of artistic quality and audience appeal. The ten films nominated for Best Picture at the Academy Awards are all still considered classics:

Dark Victory
Gone with the Wind
Goodbye, Mr. Chips
Love Affair
Mr. Smith Goes to Washington
Of Mice and Men
Stagecoach
The Wizard of Oz
Wuthering Heights
and
Ninotchka.

The movie site *Film School Rejects* laments that the glut of brilliant films in 1939 has made *Ninotchka* a 'neglected masterpiece'. Unlike the Best Picture–winning *Gone with the Wind*, which featured famous location shoots and was screened in 'Glorious Technicolor!', *Ninotchka* was a small, old-fashioned studio picture shot on the Hollywood back-lots in black and white, perhaps the perfect medium for Greta's face.

Ninotchka is often regarded as Greta's 'comeback film', reconfiguring her public image from the cool aloofness she was known for to someone who, as my mother might have said, had finally 'climbed down off her high horse and got real'. A woman who didn't just smile, but laughed! Who guffawed! Who spluttered with uncontrollable mirth! By the end of the '30s, the decade of the Great Depression, its slow recovery and the onset of war in Europe, her smile's absence and languid physicality had become a liability. The public no longer wanted aloof, idealised, aspirational heroines, but more relatable, modern, embodied women, who could, if needed, wield a rifle or heavy machinery in the coming conflicts.

Garbo needed a hit and Ernst Lubitsch, the director of such caustic and brilliant frivolities as *To Be or Not to Be*, *Bluebeard's Eighth Wife* and *Heaven Can Wait*, created one especially for her. The very catchphrase of the film's publicity campaign was *Garbo laughs!* They might as well have said: *Garbo becomes like one of us!*

I could have told them, even as an eleven-year-old, that Garbo, the divine Miss G, my Greta, was not one of us. She was something to consult as one would an oracle, not to discover, spluttering, right next to you.

Nevertheless, Garbo laughs in *Ninotchka*, as a surrender to the sensual pleasures of Paris, the debonair charm of a lover, the heady temptations of capitalism, and the lure of a ridiculous hat, all played out in proximity to the Eiffel Tower and Maxim's. In this cartoonish depiction of Paris, she comes in from the cold of her perfection with her laugh. *Ninotchka* and her laughter were to signify the apotheosis of her career, but two years later she retired from cinema and never made another film. Laughter, it seemed, could both resurrect and destroy.

*

Eventually the weather did change. While I waited for spring, I went often to the Forum des Images and reacquainted myself with the magic of sound and light. I watched Fred Astaire and Ginger Rogers dance on rollerskates; Fred, in an epic solo, danced up the walls. It may have been trick photography, but while I was watching him dancing on the ceiling I truly believed he had defied the laws of gravity. I also watched Woody Allen's *Midnight in Paris*, for which my friend Anne had done the production design. I watched the Marx Brothers go crazy in *Duck Soup*, Humphrey Bogart in love with Ingrid Bergman in *Casablanca*, and Garbo die in *Camille*. Without really noticing it, my body started to soften in the warmer days, and sleeping became easier, as the charm of Paris revealed itself.

One evening, I went in search of perfume and lipstick to bring home as presents. Since my arrival, I had avoided the quintessential tourist ritual of going to the Champs-Élysées. Infirmed by the cold, I stayed around the Marais area, which became like a village – my village, I thought, with its cobblestones and sandstones and blue and white street signs. The Champs-Élysées was the other Paris, the dream Paris, where tourists went to discover their fantasy of the city, in the glittering designer shops, under the perfectly coiffed trees, or among the handsome waiters and their imperious ways, acting as if they were the President of France more than the new Socialist president ever would.

Finding presents wasn't as simple as it once was, though. Dior had been out of the question ever since its head designer, John Galliano, had made anti-Semitic remarks at a kosher café in the Marais. Guerlain had been crossed off the list too, after its namesake CEO had made remarks about '*les nègres*' in a television interview. Chanel and Fendi were suspect because they employed Karl Lagerfeld, who was not only pro-fur but had insulted overweight women as being unhealthy and ugly. So instead of visiting the big perfumeries along the boulevard, I sought out the smaller shops in the Arcades des Champs-Élysées, searching for an unknown scent or lipstick that I could take home and announce as a true Parisian discovery. As I headed towards the arcades, I walked past a dimly lit movie memorabilia shop called Images des Antiquités and saw in the window, between photographs of Steve McQueen and Audrey Hepburn, an image of Greta I had once seen in *The Allure of Garbo*.

It was a shot from the film *Mata Hari*, in which Greta played a treacherous and glamorous spy. In it she looked away and down from the camera; her hands cradled her face; her profile all sharp edges and sleek angles. A web of lashes veiled her eyes. Her face was a perfect white mask, her mouth a dark gleaming slit.

Her face of course had not changed. A photograph never ages: that's what it does best; it remembers something perfectly. My face, on the other hand, had aged; it was already sagging slightly, its cheeks no longer rosy, its skin dulled by the cold, sleepless struggle of Paris.

I remembered this exact image because of a terrible thing I had done when I was eleven and a half. It was as if Paris, with its insistence on memory, had drawn my shame out of the forgotten crypts where I had consigned it like the rotting skulls piled high in the underground corridors beneath the city.

My family had returned home from a holiday on the Gold Coast to find that my father and I had been called to the Toowong library. Dad thought it might be for a book that hadn't been returned, or an overdue fine perhaps. He was presented, however, with a violation of what he regarded as the sanctity of a book. On the counter of the returns section, between my father and the head librarian, was *The Allure of Garbo*, with a page cut out.

Though it was comically obvious I was the culprit, I didn't confess to the crime. Then. Or ever. So the facts of the violation have remained hidden: that I couldn't take the book with me on our beach holiday; and that I couldn't bear the thought of not having it for a whole month. That the week before we left for the Gold Coast I had taken the book out for my normal weekly loan and, using one of my father's razor blades, I had carefully sliced out a page with one of my favourite pictures of Greta's inscrutable face: the one from *Mata Hari*.

I thought no one would notice it missing. It was just one face among a hundred faces, and I only needed one face to sustain me through our holiday. But an eagle-eyed librarian had noticed it gone and brought the vandalism to the attention of the head librarian. I could tell by her outrage towards me, mitigated only a little by the obvious pity she had for the parent of such a monster, that she took the transgression personally. As did my father.

Perhaps if it had been Shakespeare whose image I had cut from the binding, there might have been some indulgent smiling about my precociousness. But a glamour shot of an old actress? That seemed inexplicable.

I would have to be punished. Of course. Witnessing my father's humiliation felt like enough punishment for me, but the librarian chose to teach me a lesson by threatening to incinerate the book. Whether she went through with it or not, the immolation of the book seemed to symbolise the dreams of my life so far going up in flames.

My mother found me the next day curled up in bed crying.

Why did you do it? she asked. *It's not like a magazine that you can just tear the page out* – something she did all the time with recipes or knitting patterns.

Through the fringe of my wet lashes, Mum's face was

almost beatific. We would fight for so much of my future but no matter what I did, what changes I made, I would never ever be as naturally pretty as my mother.

I was too ashamed to tell her. I really was. But I got the words out anyway.

I'll never be beautiful.

Being beautiful isn't everything, you know. In the end it's hardly anything at all.

It's not what I wanted to hear. I wanted her to tell me there was hope for me. But she was too practical to massage my vanity. I tried to explain.

I just wanted … I just needed, I spluttered, as she rested her hand on my shoulder, *something different … something to hope for. So I wouldn't feel so hopeless and weird and … and ugly.*

I wasn't supposed to worry about such trivial things. We were too practical, too sensible for that. We put our heads down, accepted what the good Lord gave us, did our work and got on with things. That's how we survived, people like us. But I wanted to be able to look at something, settle my gaze on somebody and feel that there was somewhere to rest, to think, to contemplate, to be contemplated. I needed to believe that something magical had a place in the world – in the real world, as well as the invented world of film and movie stars.

We all like to wish upon a star, Mum said then, completely out of character. Or at least the character I knew.

I just needed … I just need, I sobbed.

You have to learn not to give in to your needs. You don't need a picture out of a book. You don't know anything about this woman's life. You think things mean something when perhaps they don't mean anything at all.

I don't need to know. I just want to look, I told her as she sighed and left the room to serve out dinner for the rest of the family. *It makes me feel hopeful when I look … that's all. Like looking at the sky at night. You can see shapes in the stars.*

*

On the sand that stretched alongside Tallebudgera Creek, you could lie down at night and really see the sky full of stars. In the lights of the galaxies, we would discover all kinds of things the Ancient Greeks might have seen: archers, scorpions, warriors, the head of Medusa, other gods and goddesses. We also saw things that made sense to us: shopping trolleys, saucepans, a teapot, the face of a wombat, the bushie who lived in a caravan at the back of the creek, an old woman's toes. I never saw Garbo's face in the stars, though, no matter how hard I looked, or how much I wanted to see it there.

You take for granted things like a sky full of stars until you live, even for a short while, in a place like Paris. Despite its beauty, and the multitude of lights and lanterns, you can't look up and see a wide, sparkling vista. The French, some say, are perhaps too explicit for the cosmic. Their language lets them go only so far, reined in by a specificity that lends itself to critical thinking and analysis, rather than flights of fancy among the heavens. Whether that's true or not, the French love their human stars, their own as well as the glamour queens of early Hollywood, whom they honour as mavericks, revolutionaries and artists.

Roland Barthes once wrote that Greta Garbo's face 'plunged audiences into the deepest ecstasy'. He continued:

> The name given to her, the Divine, probably aimed to convey less a superlative state of beauty than the essence of her corporeal person, descended from a heaven where all things are formed and perfected in the clearest light. She herself knew this ... the essence was not to be degraded, her face was not to have any reality except that of its perfection ... The Essence became gradually obscured, progressively veiled with dark glasses, broad hats and exiles: but it never deteriorated ... [Garbo's face] assures the fragile passage from awe to charm.

I recognised in Barthes' words what I had felt as a child, what I had needed to feel: a sense of wonder that such a face, and all the ideas and hope it suggested, could exist in the world; and that by looking at pictures in a book I could share that sense of wonder with other admirers from all over the world.

I had decided to Google Greta while I was in Paris. In contrast to Barthes' ode to Garbo's face, the British writer Zadie Smith saw something completely different in Garbo's aura. She wrote about Greta's existential depression and universal ennui, while describing her face as nature's work of art. Another anonymous blogger described her in later life as a thin, dour Swedish woman. I was shocked to read that after Garbo had retired from glamour she had aged ordinarily. But the most striking thing I came across was Greta's own words as she remembered herself as a young girl of eleven in Sweden:

> It was eternally grey – those long winter's nights. My father would be sitting in a corner, scribbling figures on a newspaper. On the other side of the room my mother is repairing ragged old clothes, sighing. We children would be talking in very low voices, or just sitting silently. We are filled with anxiety, as if there is danger in the air ... I was always sad as a child, for as long as I can think back.

*

About halfway through my swim across Tallebudgera Creek, my legs stopped working. My flippers felt like dead weight in the water and my goggles dug into my eyes.

I don't know to this day if it was cramp or fatigue. But my body seemed to have arrived at its limits and I was unable to continue kicking. Panicked, I gasped for air as I willed my energy down to my feet. I don't know if help was near or if my father was watching from the shore, because I had set off without telling him what I was trying to do. I had grown impatient with his training, as I often did in those days, and I knew that if I had told him I wanted to try to cross on my own he would have warned me to wait, to practise more.

As my arms began to weaken and my head began to slip under the water, I had the idea to flip myself onto my back and float on the water. After a couple of tries, I managed to do this, arranging and rearranging my body so it was balanced on the water's surface.

From that angle it seemed extraordinary how the sun filled the sky, the way its rays washed the clouds in amber light. Squinting and opening my eyes in rapid succession, like the camera's eye opening and closing as it films, I thought the sky no longer looked like a sky, but a whole world of messages and signs, a blue and yellow page on which was written the story of my life, with all the things I had done, all the things I would do and dream, and all the things I would fail to do.

As I looked up, my arms began to rotate at my sides, so that my body spun slowly in the water. Though I felt that I held this position for a long time, it would have been only a minute or so that I floated this way on my back. But it was a minute in which the world seemed filled with endless possibilities, a minute in which I lost my panic and my fear, in which I calmed down and found my strength again.

After that minute ended, I felt my confidence return. I flipped back over onto my stomach, arced my arms above my head, as I had practised for so many years, and began to swim. Gently at first, then faster and stronger, I churned through the rippling waves until I reached the sand at the other side of the creek, where to my surprise my father was waiting for me with a towel and a Paddle Pop. He was inscrutable as always, and it was hard to tell whether he was angry or impressed. His sense of calm was, as usual, possibly misleading, and I wondered whether he had witnessed my swim from a protective distance. Or whether he had just left me to it, as he would so often in my life.

*

The screening of *Ninotchka* at the Forum des Images was in late July, a month before I was due to leave Paris. I had never seen the film and was excited to see it in the city where it was set. On my way to the Forum, I dropped in at Starbucks near the Hôtel de Ville and ordered the same tea latte I'd been drinking every day since I arrived in February. As I was about to leave, I saw Mathilde sitting at my favourite spot near the window. At least I thought it was Mathilde: she looked completely different. Her once radiant face was pinched and tense, as if she were suffering in some way, although I couldn't tell whether it was physical, mental or emotional.

I hurt my back, she told me when I asked her how she was. *I was reaching up to examine a painting at the Louvre and I felt something snap. Apparently it's a muscle spasm. You should have seen me a month ago, I was wearing a back brace. All bent over like the Hunchback of Notre Dame.*

She laughed.

I sat down opposite her. I didn't know how to help her, this beautiful Parisian girl who now looked so worn and damaged. I asked her what therapies she was using to help her recover.

It's not the best city to recover in, she grimaced. *The best thing of course is swimming. But it's hard to find a pool that's not full of people at this time of year. We suffer for so long in the cold that we kind of go crazy in the summer. We pack everything we can into those few warm months, because we know what's ahead is the long winter. Do you swim?*

We all learn as children in Australia, I said. *It's too dangerous not to. Swimming might help your back, I think.*

I never learned properly, you know. All I do is paddle like a little dog. But at least I'm in the water.

We talked a bit longer. She told me how she planned to go to the sea if she could, to Brittany or Normandy. Or, if she managed to get some money together, perhaps to Marseilles or Saint-Tropez.

Or maybe you can invite me to Australia, she teased. *I hear it's gorgeous there, even in winter.*

It's the best time to be there. The sun's out, the sky is blue and there's just a little nip in the air.

Sounds perfect. She sighed, rearranging herself carefully in the chair. *You should write for your country's tourist department.*

Maybe I should. But when I'm there for too long, I always want to leave. It's like a puzzle I'm always trying to solve. This pull and push of where I come from.

Sounds like a luxurious puzzle to have, she mused.

By the way, I'm sorry we didn't meet up at the Louvre, I said. *I just got really down in the cold and kind of turned in on myself.*

I felt bad about that. Another lost opportunity, I thought. Another possible connection with a human being, ruined by my obsessions.

It's called hibernation, she reassured me. *Anyway, there's still time. That's what we have a lot of in Paris. We have time. The past. The present.*

And the future?

Not so much, she laughed again. *Look around us. We may as well be living in a museum. It drives you crazy sometimes, all that stone and dust. That's why a lot of young people want to leave. To find the future. But we think if we make time for time, the future will take care of itself.*

I went back to the counter and ordered a coffee for her. Just to say thanks. I asked for the most voluptuous coffee they had in the house. A double mocha with double cream and two spoons of chocolate sprinkled on top. She was delighted when I brought it to her.

I call it the Mathilde, I said. *It's the most beautiful coffee I could think of. It's my way of saying thanks to a beautiful girl from Paris.*

What for? She looked puzzled and even a little teary. *Look around you. This city is full of beautiful girls. Believe me, I'm nothing special.*

Well, first of all, thanks for telling me about the Forum des Images. I'm heading there now.

Oh, what's on?

A Greta Garbo film called Ninotchka.

Where she laughs? she squealed delightedly. *It's a classic.*

You've seen it?

I've seen a lot of her films, she said, matter-of-fact. *We watched some in Film Studies. And, of course, most philosophy students know the essay Barthes wrote about her face. Superb!*

I couldn't hide my surprise.

What's so amusing? she asked, noticing my wry smile.

I laughed. *Just having a Paris moment.*

And second of all? she prompted me.

Second of all, I echoed. *Thanks for reminding me of something I thought I'd forgotten. Or at least missed out on.*

Which is? she quizzed me, curious.

Paris. I thought I'd failed in Paris, because all I've really done is stay in my room remembering things from my past.

That's what winters are for, she said. *Everything goes dark and everything dies. Then spring comes, and there are little glimmers of hope; then summer, and everything comes to life. That's what we do in Paris. We understand seasons and time. People come and go, but here we are, a memorial to memory and time.*

I stood up to go. I didn't want to be late for the film, as I had often been. I was tired of seeing the exasperated face of the cashier at the cinema when I arrived, panting and late, at the counter.

Mathilde laughed again when I explained the reason for my haste, then lifted her mocha coffee and toasted her city. *To Paris then.*

Yes, I echoed as I turned to leave. *To Paris.*

*

I did arrive late at the Forum after my unexpected meeting with Mathilde. I bought my ticket for *Ninotchka* from the disapproving cashier, who refused to leave his post to guide me into the darkened cinema. As I picked my way across bodies to find an empty seat, I felt disorientated after the bright warmth of my day, momentarily blind in the absence of light.

Five minutes or so after I had settled into my seat, the night scenes of the film abruptly switched to daylight as Greta Garbo, her face grim and determined, strode across a room. I suddenly realised I was surrounded by hundreds of Parisian film-lovers, laughing at the comic actors to whom Greta was playing the 'straight man'. As I listened to the laughter, I recalled again that sense of wonder and mystery I had felt as a child, that something luminous and magical was touching me. I remembered the young girl I'd been, poring over my copy of *A Pictorial History of the Movies*, and *The Allure of Garbo*, while my mother knocked on the door and told me not to read too much or stay up too late, that there was a big world out there and reading about films and staring at exotic faces was not going to give me the tools to get on in life. And, as sometimes happens, I felt time move downward as well as forward: I became aware of textures and meanings that had been hidden from view. I could finally see the vast distance I had crossed in my life, geographically and metaphorically, in order to have arrived there in Les Halles, watching Greta Garbo finally laugh on screen.

The actual scene where *Garbo laughs!* was pure slapstick. Her would-be lover is determined to charm her out of her seriousness and into his bed. I imagine many others had tried and failed throughout Greta's cinematic life to arouse her in a similar way, to carry her down into the earth, to make her 'normal', grounded, one of us. Her lover accidentally falls out of a chair. Humiliated, he prepares to lift himself back up, but then looks across and sees Garbo laughing and laughing. It is like ice thawing.

The warmth of summer took a long time to arrive in Paris that year, but when I walked outside the cinema after *Ninotchka* ended, Les Halles was shining in golden light. The cold had finally passed and for me, and for many in the city, there was a reason to smile again. As I walked back to my studio, I thought once more of the young girl I had been in the summer between my eleventh and twelfth birthdays, kicking and gasping across Tallebudgera Creek to get from one side to the other, so that at the end of the long struggle I could look back across the dark expanse of water and time to see that the place where I had started out was just a shimmering speck on the horizon. After months of bitter cold, I felt a tide of warmth, love and hope overwhelm me in the balmy air of Paris. I wondered whether all of us marvel at times about how we get here, as I had that evening in the cinema, while on a black-and-white screen a thin, dour Swedish woman laughed and laughed.

On Kindness in Kolkata

The airline official at Kolkata's Dum Dum airport hardly glanced at me, even though he appeared to be smiling, as he told me my backpack had been left on the Danish Air plane from which I had disembarked just after midnight.

I'm afraid it is on its way to Copenhagen, miss.

Copenhagen? I repeated incredulously.

Yes, miss, I believe it is in Denmark.

I was too flabbergasted to reply that I knew where Copenhagen was. I was more concerned with how I was going to get my things back to the subcontinent and, more immediately, how I was going to survive in Kolkata with only two books of travellers' cheques, a toothbrush and a passport secreted in my bum bag. In my giddy excitement at embarking on my first overseas solo adventure, I'd imagined skipping out of the airport into the steamy

Kolkata night with my bum bag around my hips, my pack on my back, and a subcontinental siren's song in my heart.

Instead, I was deflated as I slumped into the nearest available chair and looked around for someone to commiserate with. There was one other friendly-looking westerner in the building, a middle-aged priest who was sitting in the departure area, reading what I assumed was a prayer book. I introduced myself and discovered his name was Father Maurice; after volunteering for a year in India he was heading home to his parish in Malta. Father Maurice invited me to join him while I waited to fill in my lost-luggage papers. *It might take a while*, he winked knowingly.

It did. At around 6 am, officials from the airline arrived to take my report and assure me the luggage would be returned ASAP, and that in the meantime reparations would be made to help clothe me.

Meeting Father Maurice was fortuitous for more than just the gift of his company. As I walked with him to his departure gate, he suggested I take a rickshaw straight to the YWCA, in the heart of the city – it would be the safest place for a young woman travelling alone.

I took Father Maurice's advice and, after a hair-raising trip by rickshaw through the early-morning mists, arrived at the YWCA. So I have Danish Air, Father Maurice and my delayed lost luggage to thank for my subsequent encounter with the women of the Y and the various hospitals run by Mother Teresa's Missionaries of Charity in Kolkata, at which many of these women volunteered while they lived in the city.

It's said people go to India for a number of reasons: they come to climb the mountains, to simmer in the deserts, to embrace hedonism on the southern beaches; they come for the ancient mysteries, for the colour and sound, for the buildings and monuments; they come for the gurus, yogis and sadhus, to find spirituality in the ashrams.

I'd come for none of those reasons.

I'd headed to Kolkata to satisfy my sense of adventure and curiosity about the world. I intended to travel around India for six months before going to Europe, and Kolkata was my first port of call: there seemed no more adventurous place to begin than the so-called city of joy. At first it seemed impossible to find joy in this place of beggars and corpulent billionaires. But it was there, I found, waiting in the most unexpected places.

I had come without plans or maps, meaning to stay a few days or a week at the most. But I lived in the city for nearly two months as I waited for my luggage to be returned. Meanwhile, I dressed myself in Indian clothes from the market bazaar across the road from the Y, where I got to know its assortment of guests.

They were a diverse bunch: there was Gloria, the Texan millionaire, roughing it at the YWCA while answering God's call as a volunteer at Mother Teresa's hospital, helping babies with tuberculosis. She used to take photos of the shower faucets to send back home to her millionaire buddies, to prove, I suppose, that she really was 'roughing it'. There was the lovely, lithe Amy from Dorchester, who'd arrived in Kolkata after volunteering for six months at an Israeli kibbutz. She spent her days working at one of the hospitals and her evenings fraternising with US marines at the local army base. There was middle-aged Hilary from Sussex, with her carefully coiffed hair and peaches-and-cream complexion, a follower of the notorious Sai Baba. She was staying at the Y for mysterious reasons, as far as I knew.

Most intriguing were Helga and Gretchen, the spoiled cousins from Berlin, whose industrialist fathers had sent them to Kolkata for an all-expenses-paid reality check. After their mandatory work with the Missionaries each morning, they would spend the afternoon getting manicures and pedicures by the pool in a five-star hotel.

Prior to my landing in Kolkata, all my travel had been with orchestras. I was used to the security of friends, and it was not hard for me to make connections. In Kolkata, it started with the simple act of sharing food in the sparse dining room of the YWCA. At first the ladies found it amusing to watch me navigate my way around all the chillies and spices, and I played along genially, happy to begin our communications with the shared laugh over my inability to comfortably consume even the relatively mild

Bengali food. Amy spoke to me first. She was curious as to why I had turned up on the first evening wearing traditional Punjabi Indian clothes, a long tunic over billowing pants. I told her the story of my luggage, which was, I assumed, now safely in Copenhagen. She regaled the others with the story of my new Indian wardrobe and soon we were all chortling at the surprises of travel.

I shared the next few evening meals with the group as I slowly acclimatised to the startling stimulation of Kolkata and its smoggy chaos. Gradually I found out the stories of Gloria, Gretchen and Helga, Hilary and Amy, and by the fourth evening I had been invited to accompany them the next morning on their way to the hospital where they were all volunteering.

We started the day early with breakfast in the dining room. Amy spooned chilli jam out of a jar. I was aghast but impressed by her fortitude, but she had been in India for six months, she explained, and she was determined to have the full Indian experience. And if that meant re-educating her Anglo-Saxon digestive system, so be it. The others ate porridge as I did. I had two bowls, sensing I would need extra nourishment for the day ahead. Hilary left us then; she was going to take a rickshaw to the hospital that morning.

After breakfast we all gathered outside the YWCA, where we were surrounded by child beggars, some of them on makeshift skateboards. It was not the first time I had witnessed such things. Usually as I walked down the streets of Kolkata, I was followed by several beggars. But our small group attracted a crowd of them, multiplying the shock. Amy, who seemed to be the natural leader of the group, spoke cheerfully to the children and gave each of them a small cake she had secreted in her pockets. She treated them as equals, as children just like any other children. I could see how the other women looked to Amy, and the way she interacted with the beggars, as an example of how to overcome their own discomfort.

When she stepped out ahead of the group and began to lead us all down the street, it seemed appropriate that we all fell in behind her. Gloria chatted in her broad American accent. Helga and Gretchen studiously picked their way around the more obvious piles of dirt and refuse that were strewn across the footpath. Amy seemed to know where she was going, so I happily joined in the group as we made our way to the hospital. We came to a corner where we all stopped. An old woman wrapped in plastic lay propped up against a street light. Amy kneeled down beside her and kissed her on the cheek. The woman beamed and spoke what I assumed was rapid Bengali. *This is Priyanka*, Amy called out to me. *Priyanka, this is Linda. She's lost all her luggage but she's not lost now that we've found her.* Gloria went to buy some curd for Priyanka as I kneeled down beside Amy and took the old woman's hand. *She's lived here for years*, Amy told me, *on this corner. The plastic helps keep her warm in winter. She has nothing but somehow*

she's survived because of the kindness of passers-by. Gloria
kneeled down with us and began to spoon-feed the curd to
Priyanka out of a pottery bowl. It felt strangely intimate to
be part of the group around this old woman, who lived on
a street corner in a third-world city.

After a few more minutes we started off along the road
again. As Amy called out to Priyanka that she would see
her again the next morning, I looked back to see the old
woman talking to others around her. Some paid attention, others didn't. Around the next corner, we passed a
line of up to a hundred women holding babies on their
hips or children by the hand. They were waiting for the
food donations given out twice a day by the Missionaries
of Charity. Amy explained all this to me as we made our
way to the entrance. Despite the activities around us, there
was a distinctive sense of calm and peace in the building.
Mother Teresa wasn't there that day, nor any of the other
days I worked at the hospital. She was in Bangladesh at the
time, setting up an aid program for the poor.

Mother Teresa prompted ambivalence in India. Some
educated Bengalis I met opposed her stance on contra-
ception, and were incensed by her Christianity in this
Hindu-majority country. Others thought she was a saint.

The work I saw and participated in was sincere and
worthwhile. I held tiny babies in my hand who had been
rescued from rubbish bins, watched nuns and volunteers
nurse sick infants back to health, and witnessed some

children die. Despite the distress I saw many inspiring things in the Kolkata hospitals.

I wasn't as committed as the others, and didn't go every day. Sometimes I attended the Bible reading group at the YWCA. Other times, I consulted my 'other bible', the *Lonely Planet Travel Guide to India*, which I had studied before I left Australia. I learned from the *Lonely Planet Guide* that Kolkata had a coterie of India's top writers, filmmakers and artists, and that Bengal was the home of India's great poet Tagore. I also learned place names like the Hooghly district and Howrah station. I visited both. I caught the train to Darjeeling and attended poetry readings. But mainly I hung around the Y with my new friends, who were truly committed to their volunteer work.

On one of the days I accompanied them to the hospital, I met a Bengali social worker, Sonja, who introduced me to her family of teachers and intellectuals, with whom I shared several home-cooked meals. Sonja's family taught me many things, including how to eat dinner with my hands, how to dress in a sari and how to pray for miracles. They were devout Christians and counted Mother Teresa as a close family friend. They credited her with a miracle they told me to believe in: their youngest son dying from cancer had fully recovered after months of prayer directed towards his healing.

I told Amy of this miracle. She shrugged. I thought she was unimpressed. *We see miracles every day*, she told me, *each equal to the other.* I sensed in her demeanour that she would go on to live a magnificent life, so open was she to the everyday opportunities to help, to laugh, to share and to love.

The nuns at the hospital were also open to such things. They weren't overly effusive, but they were tender when they needed to be. I witnessed such tenderness one day when I watched a tiny nun wrapped in the white robes of the Missionaries of Charity hold in her small hand a premature baby no bigger than the size of her outstretched fingers. With her other hand, she stroked the baby's cheek and stomach. Back home in Australia, such a fragile infant would live for months in intensive care, supported by tubes and oxygen, and myriad hospital staff. But in Kolkata, there was only human touch to keep the baby alive. Amy understood this too, and she spent hours with the nun and the infant, gently laying her hand on the baby, giving through touch the hope of life.

After my luggage finally arrived, I headed south to what I hoped would be an unforgettable adventure. But I felt I had left a part of my heart back in the fumes and chaos of West Bengal's capital.

I circumnavigated the subcontinent, stopping first in Chennai, and moving south to the temple town of Madurai, ending up in the coastal town of Kollam, in Kerala – the Indian state with the highest literacy rate. From there I embarked on a three-day train trip back up to New Delhi, where I swam in a pool at the Raj Club, went to the Red Fort, and met a tall Sikh man who asked me to smuggle diamonds into Pakistan. I declined. I then flew to London and would go on to spend the summer in Europe, but first I was marooned for a week in an isolation ward in an infectious-diseases hospital. It was dysentery: I didn't write home about this adventure, not wanting to worry my parents, but when I finally got over the bug, I celebrated by eating double meals for a fortnight.

By the end of the year I had returned to Brisbane. I re-established myself far too easily, as if the previous year had hardly happened at all. I taught violin and worked free-lance as an orchestral musician. But my grandmother could tell I was restless. *She's caught the travel bug*, she said to my mother, as if it were a disease from which I would take many years to recover.

I made secret plans to travel again. High on my list of places to revisit was Kolkata, even though I could hardly find the words to describe my experiences to the people I knew in Brisbane. My vocabulary had not expanded enough to express what was still then the inexpressible. I missed the city, I missed the crowds, the animals, the endless stimulation – even the dirt and the proximity of life to death. I had seen how the kindness of strangers could keep hope alive, longer than you thought possible.

Despite many plans, I did not return to the city. My

memory of it is still intense, however – perhaps because I never went back. The city is embedded in my skin, in my ears, my nose, my eyes and my heart.

I will, for instance, never forget an afternoon I spent at Kalighat, where incurably ill people were cared for as long as they needed. After a morning spent sunning myself by the pool with Helga and Gretchen, I visited the hospice, where I stayed beside the cot of an old woman recently taken off the street. Her hips had been broken and left untreated so often that her bones now jutted through the skin. As she called out in rasping Bengali, the Missionaries of Charity came to her with water, food and resolute tenderness.

In the dimming light I watched these softly smiling carers soothing the dying woman and, by doing so, allowing her to die with some dignity.

I never again travelled with the *Lonely Planet Guide* to anywhere and learned that travel was best unplanned. After all, it was a mishap that made me stay in the city longer than I intended. I am still grateful to Danish Air, to the smiling official at Dum Dum airport, to my lost luggage in Copenhagen, to Father Maurice and the eccentric women of the Y that I was there to witness those moments in the dusty afternoon light of Kolkata.

Notes from the Musical Frontier

In the early '90s, I was still a classical musician, though I'd played in a band with my boyfriend in Brisbane. After we broke up I set off for Sydney to escape the drama, and to find a new kind of life, as you sometimes do in those defining moments of love or heartbreak.

Classical music had already provided me a chance to see the world: as a student I'd played Shostakovich in the Roman Forum, right next door to the Colosseum; performed *Peter and the Wolf* in London to Peter Ustinov's narration; and attended the Festival of Youth Orchestras in Aberdeen, where young musicians from places as diverse as Venezuela and Sweden performed concertos and symphonies near the misty Scottish forests.

I loved the classical repertoire and appreciated the technical discipline it gave me. But after a stint as a freelance violinist for opera, ballet and chamber orchestras and string quartets, I was ready for some musical adventures. I was looking for opportunities, I suppose, that would help me develop from the competent professional I was trained to be into something looser, more creative and free.

I was living on Sydney's north shore, yet to make my move into the inner city, when I heard a song on the radio by Australian guitarist and songwriter Ed Kuepper – 'The Way I Made You Feel'. I didn't know much about Ed. I'd probably been going to Musica Viva concerts, listening to Beethoven string quartets and playing beginner's Bach when he was creating The Saints, arguably one of the world's first punk bands, in his parents' garage in Oxley, a few suburbs further west from where I'd grown up in St Lucia. We came from two different musical worlds, but I heard something in his song that really struck me: a space in its sound – a space for a violin, perhaps.

I soon found out more about Ed: that The Saints had disbanded after a flurry of stardom in the late '70s; that he had gone on to create and front more celebrated indie groups, including the post-punk experimental band Laughing Clowns, The Aints and The Yard Goes On Forever. 'The Way I Made You Feel' was from the ARIA Award–nominated album *Honey Steel's Gold*, and marked a new surge in popularity for Ed and his songwriting.

Shortly after hearing the song, I moved to Newtown, at the heart of Sydney's inner west. In those days, Newtown was gritty and dynamic, home to performance artists, singers, musos, comics and actors, as well as a colourful assortment of ratbags and desperadoes, all vibrating with creative hopes and schemes. I started playing with a number of bands in the evenings, improvising and orchestrating string parts, and busking in Kings Cross and various places across town during the days. This generated most of my income: I couldn't calculate the number of hot meals I bought courtesy of Vivaldi's *Four Seasons* and Mozart's *Eine Kleine Nachtmusik*.

I'd pretty much forgotten my idea of playing with Ed when one day I passed him in the porridge aisle of the local supermarket. Knowing he lived locally inspired me to try to give him a recording of my music, in the hope he might like the idea of having a violin play on his songs.

I didn't know of any formal ways to approach him. I asked a few people in the area what they thought of me knocking on his door, or slipping my tape into his mailbox. Everyone said it was a bad idea. He was known to be somewhat aloof and didn't suffer fools at all. So I let the idea rest for a while. In the meantime I seemed to hear his music everywhere: on the radio, in bars and cafés.

Busking wasn't a reliable source of income, and like many other musos I had to resort to the dole to tide me over when work was scarce. One lunch hour, I was on my way to Social Security in the arcade near Newtown station when I saw Ed. He was heading towards me, accompanied by two young men I assumed were in his band. It seemed so fortuitous that our paths were about to intersect that I stopped right in front of him, summoned up my courage and asked if he thought he'd ever need a violinist on his songs. I expected him to live up to his reputation and walk on by with a look of disdain. Instead he smiled at me and asked if I had a business card. I didn't.

He suggested I send him something. If I had a pen and paper, he would give me his PO box address. All I had was a Social Security envelope and a lipstick in my back pocket. He seemed dubious, but tolerant, as I used them to write down his address and put the lipstick-smeared paper back into my pocket. He said he'd get in touch when he'd listened to my demos.

I didn't expect this encounter to come to anything, but I sent off the recordings and waited. And waited and waited. A couple of months later, out of the blue, I received a call from Ed. He asked if I was available for a recording in a couple of weeks at EMI's Studios 301 in town. I was. Of course. After one rehearsal session, I turned up one evening and played on a new version of the classic Australian song 'Sad Dark Eyes'. It was for *Earth Music*, a charity album in support of the environment. The recording took hours and we stayed at the studio well into the night. Other musicians became irritable and bored with the delays, but I was thrilled with the new experience. Learning about the art of recording, something I felt would be significant for my future, was a bonus. Despite Ed's generally inscrutable personality, I enjoyed the process and felt I'd found a kind of entrée into a brave new musical world.

After 'Sad Dark Eyes' came out, I played with Ed on and off during the next couple of years. There were many highlights. Our second recording together – another cover, 'If I Had a Ticket' – reached the Triple J Top Ten. We went on tours around Australia and New Zealand, performing with Crowded House at the Hordern Pavilion, with The Cruel Sea at the Big Backyard, and to a crowd of 1200 at the old Phoenician Club on Broadway.

We also played to seven people in a small bar in New Zealand, and to a hostile crowd in Newcastle, where old punks yelled at Ed to play his Saints songs. I got some idea from those gigs how tough it must have been in the early days of punk, with its alcohol-fuelled aggression and rowdy anti-authoritarianism, often levelled at the performers as much as anyone else. Sometimes out-of-it punters would lay their heads on the bass amps at the front of the stage, and I worried – in my decidedly non-punk way – about their hearing. Once I fell off the edge of the stage while backing away from a crowd surge. Ed found it funny. So did I. Kind of. And alarming too.

I never really got used to the intense volume of his shows but eventually enjoyed the raw freedom of improvising on electric violin. Along with the grinding, sometimes primitive rhythms, there were interludes of surprisingly sweet songs:

'I Wish You Were Here', with which we used to end most shows; and an acoustic version of 'The Way I Made You Feel'.

This wasn't the music or the performing conditions I had grown used to in the classical world, where the chairs are set up for you in neat rows, where rehearsals start on time and performances end respectably early – and where you are paid union rates. This was music on the frontier, music in the wild. I also saw up close the highs and lows of being an independent musician in Australia, in the days when having a career meant performing live as much as you could. I marvelled at Ed's tenacity in the face of criticism, how much his dogged self-belief made him keep going when others would have folded.

I discovered some unexpected things about Ed: he had an almost encyclopaedic appreciation of pop music's history, an extraordinary vinyl collection, and the type of loyal fans who would follow his musical odysseys no matter where they took him – or them. I also observed how a long musical career did not always equate to popularity, and that the point sometimes was to just keep going.

I never really got to know Ed, though, and sometimes we approached each other like we were different species of aliens. He thought I was a bit of a musical princess, while I sometimes imagined him as a soldier facing down the enemy with his blaring electric guitar.

One incident sums up what I learned from these experiences. The first full-length album I played on was *Character*

Assassination. As was my habit, I'd asked for recordings of the songs in advance, so that I could practise for hours and come up with parts, as I had been trained to do. But this time, for some reason, I didn't get a chance to prepare.

I was a bit nervous when I got to the studio and I asked Ed to run the tape of a song called 'The Cockfighter' so I could work something out before we recorded. As I listened to the track I fumbled along with the music, sliding my finger around the strings, searching for the right notes. Unsure of what I should play, but feeling my way as best I could, I was confident that with another couple of run-throughs I'd work out something we could use.

At the end of the song, Ed stopped the tape and asked me to go over and put some harmonies on what I'd just played. I was horrified to find out he had recorded my fumblings and intended to use them on his album. I begged him to let me record it again. He argued that no matter how hard I worked at it I would never be able to re-create what I had improvised when I thought no one was listening. When I wasn't judging myself.

Believe me, he reassured me, *people around the world whose hearts are pure will remember that part more than anything you worked out or performed well.*

I didn't know it at the time, but he was right. Even though to my ears it was full of wrong notes and weird sounds, there was something about its uncertainty that was more than just lines of music: it became what the song was about.

When the album came out, *Rolling Stone* singled out that solo as something special. I sometimes quote the review to others. Not so much to boast – after all, it was Ed, not me, who ensured my part stayed the way it was on the album – but to illustrate how musicians from different worlds can connect with each other through a song.

Sometimes there is a difference between being perfect or even good and being real and true. Maybe that's where the art happens. That day in the studio I stepped out of the safe classical world I came from, and into the wild blue musical frontierland where Ed seemed to stride, a man on an independent mission, armed with his bravado, his energy and his blazing electric guitar.

Epilogue: All Is Given

I thought I would always travel but since I was diagnosed with a chronic illness my movement has been curtailed. Sometimes getting to the end of the street is an epic journey. But I have discovered that one does not always have to travel far to find people to meet. In the last two months, I have welcomed a variety of nationalities into my home – people from Argentina, Zambia, Sudan, India. These are not travellers. Most of them are refugees who have made a home in the city where I live. They visit me as domestic assistants and, as I sit in the chair while they work, they bring the world to me while I am at present unable to go out to meet the world.

These travel stories are not complete. There are many I have left out, like the time I spent living with the grandson of a duchess in a castle near the border between Austria and Czechoslovakia. I met him in Freak Street, where many years later I met Gabriel. His name was Sigmund and, after leaving him in Kathmandu, I would eventually take the train from Waterloo station, London, to meet him in Vienna. With him I travelled in a red sports car with his grandmother the duchess up the highway from Vienna to their castle, where they lived in the old servants' quarters. It is a great story but I won't tell it here. I leave it up to you to imagine and to fill in all the blank spaces that I am now telling you I have left in this book. I also left out the time I was the only white woman in a sari on a beach in Kerala, in the south of India. I was surrounded by children that day. I was an oddity in whom they found delight. I was happy then. But I have left that story out too.

I also have not told you about the time while sitting in a room full of silent meditators in Dehradun, a town north of Rishikesh in India, I felt the earth move beneath me. Many others felt it too, and for a while some of us were convinced that our meditations had levitated us above the earth. Because it was a silent meditation retreat, it took a few hours for us to be informed that in Kashmir, over a hundred kilometres away, an earthquake had broken the surface of the country. They say ignorance is bliss, and that day it might have been true, because before we knew the facts, some of us could dream that the impossible had actually happened.

Ten years after that earthquake, another reduced the city of Kathmandu to rubble. Durbar Square and its surrounding streets were destroyed. I don't know what happened to Studio Acoustica. A small recording studio in a Buddhist square did not make the news.

Two months ago, my wise friend Sophie rang me after a long silence. She had been grieving for her sister, who died last year of leukaemia. We spoke about letting go and moving on. She told me of an old Latin saying that meant 'it is given'. We talked at length about what it meant when one could just relax into life and accept, after all the struggles, that life would give you gifts you could not imagine. These stories are the gifts that I could not have imagined. And as I have written them, I have been transported back to those places, and those times, and those people, whose hearts became entwined with mine. And I've realised that life gives you gifts even if sometimes you are looking in the other direction. And just as songs sometimes dropped out of the sky into my body, to be born as music, these stories appeared before me, to be born as this book.

As I remember the stories that I have told and have yet to tell, I remember moments of sheer joy: when I danced on a beach, when I sang to a crowd, when I held the hand of a stranger as I walked through chaos. I especially remember standing in the middle of no man's land between the borders of Austria and Czechoslovakia, when in a moment of bravado I did an Isadora Duncan dance to the invisible guards in the watchtowers. I was happy then too.

As for the specifics of the stories I have told, do you really need me to fill in the blanks? Should I tell you that five months after meeting Gabriel near a Buddhist temple, I returned to Kathmandu and recorded an album of love songs in Studio Acoustica with Bizou and all the rest of the Nepali boys who dreamed of music? I did not take photographs on that trip, although Gabriel took them of me. The record I made was in song.

*

As I've told you, I've played music in many different ways. First of all, learning violin in a nun's music room. Then playing with pianos and other violins, school orchestras, youth symphony orchestras, chamber orchestras, string quartets, string orchestras. I went electric and played in rock'n'roll bands. Then I unplugged, went acoustic again and improvised for meditators in the hills behind Byron Bay. In many ways I have travelled through music as well as through countries. When I was preparing for my lounge-room tour, I used to sit in my lounge room and play my songs in simple acoustic versions to my friend Estelle in my cottage in West End. After many years of travelling through music, playing in my lounge room to my friend felt like coming home. But it was the beginning of another journey. These stories I have told you are like songs as well, and I have found many different ways of telling them: from the fabulous to the delicate, from the bustling movement through third-world cities, to high tea in Shanghai, to a walk along the river in Paris. In ending this book, I have discovered a truly intimate way of crafting a story. Because at this moment, I am sitting in my lounge room in Brisbane, Australia, telling my story over Skype as once I sang a song to Estelle, who is typing down these words for me as she sits in her flat in California. And, despite the distance between us, the feeling is as intimate as if we were together, sitting in the same lounge room, as we once did.

Acknowledgements

It took many years to make this book, and there are many people who helped grow it along the way. First of all, thanks to University of Queensland Press for supporting the publication of this book. In particular, to my publisher, Alexandra Payne, whose unwavering and inspiring support for the book helped me finish it. To my brilliant editor, Ian See, whose insight, skill and kindness helped it become a better book than it otherwise might have been. To my agent, Clare Forster, for her guidance and care. And to Gail Jones and Zoë Morrison, for taking the time to read and respond to the manuscript before it was published.

Many friends and colleagues gave their invaluable time and support. Thanks to Wendy Foley for her wise advice and consistent friendship, and to Dr Estelle Castro-Koshy, whose generous and empathetic editorial support and practical help with typing up the manuscript were crucial in bringing this book to fruition. Sophie Pearce, Claudia Taranto, Joanne Douglas and Anna Nolan all read early versions of the manuscript. Thanks also to Ross E for his enduring love and support, Gabriel P for sharing beautiful adventures, and Maureen Strachan for encouraging me to keep going. To Martin Ma, for his enthusiastic collaboration. To my sister Janice, for her courage and inspiration, and to my generous, radiant sister Cathie, who also loves to travel. To Stephen Neil and Paul and Kym Bosley-Neil, for their ever-present laughter. And to Finn and Kel, for lighting up my life.

Thanks to the Chinese International School in Hong Kong for sponsoring my trip to Mongolia, and to the Australia Council for the Arts, Arts Queensland, AsiaLink, the Shanghai Writers' Association, ABC Radio National, the Peggy Glanville-Hicks Composers' House and EMSAH at the University of Queensland – in particular, the late Jan McKemmish, and Dr Bronwyn Lea – who all provided financial, residential and collegial support for my development as a writer.

And to all my friends, new and old, around the world, who inspired, encouraged and loved me through the years. I love you all.

Linda Neil's music is available at
http://lindaneil.bandcamp.com/releases